T95-04

T9S-04

TRANSITIONS

A Practical Guide to the Workplace

Linda Winder
Sonja Stih
Jim O'Connor

Collier Macmillan Canada, Inc.

Copyright © 1989 Collier Macmillan Canada, Inc.

Collier Macmillan Canada, Inc.
1200 Eglinton Ave. East, Suite 200,
Don Mills, Ontario
M3C 3N1

Canadian Cataloguing in Publication Data

Winder, Linda
    Transitions: a practical guide to the workplace

ISBN 0.02.953522.0

1. Work. 2. Vocational guidance. I. Stih, Sonja.
II. O'Connor, Jim, 1942–   . III. Title.

HF5381.W56 1989   650.1'4   C89–095433–X

Designer: Sarah Laffey
Editor: John Eerkes
Illustrator: ThachBùi/Artattack

Printed and bound in Canada

1 2 3 4 5 94 93 92 91 90 89

Contents

Dedication

Linda Winder

To my only daughter, Jody, who will face many transitions in the years ahead, and to my family and friends who have supported me through several transitions of my own.

Sonja Stih

To my parents who have seen me through many past transitions, and to George, with whom I plan to share many more.

Jim O'Connor

To Jamie and Sam, for the many humorous discussions we have had on exploring careers.

Preface

Today, through television, newspapers, radio, and other communications media, people are exposed to all aspects of the world. We are more aware of and knowledgeable about famines, political upheavals, medical discoveries, technological advances, and the earth's various races and cultures than any other generation in history.

How about you? Are you prepared to adapt to the new "high tech/high touch" society? How well do you know yourself? As the world becomes spaceship earth, do you feel ready to meet the challenges the future will present to you? Do you face this prospect with fear or excitement?

This book is written to help prepare you for the challenge of making the TRANSITION from school to work and to prepare you for the job market of tomorrow.

The TRANSITION from school to work is an important one. For many, it is smooth. For others, it may be a shaky passage. TRANSITIONS will assist you to make a prepared, meaningful crossover from one stage of your life to the next. Good luck!

Acknowledgments

The authors gratefully acknowledge these people in the preparation of TRANSITIONS:

- John Eerkes, Editor, for his help in the preparation of this text, and especially for his sense of humour, which made this project a fun one.

- Patrick Gallagher, Editorial Director, for his unending patience and optimism during the long writing process.

- Joanne Johnston, School Sales Manager, for her vision and enthusiasm from conception to completion.

- Linda Rou, for her research assistance.

- Our reviewers: Catherine Lang, Co-Ordinator, Co-Operative Research Centre, O.I.S.E., Toronto;   Jack Wenaus, Co-Operative Work Education, Halifax District School Board; Marjatta Longston, Co-Operative Education Co-Ordinator, Sudbury Board of Education;   Mary Cosentino, Supervisor of Co-Operative Education, Metropolitan Separate School Board, Toronto;   John Ludgate, Career Education Consultant, North Shore Continuing Education, North and West Vancouver School Districts;   George Clapham, Department of Co-Operative Education, Centennial College, Scarborough;   Bill Watson, Co-Ordinator, The City Centre Co-Operative Education School, Sault Ste. Marie;   Bernice Stebbing, Child Guidance Clinic, Winnipeg School Division No. 1, for the generous contribution of their time in reviewing the manuscript and offering their expertise and suggestions along the way.

Work Today and Tomorrow

CHAPTER 1

The Nature of Work

After completing this chapter, you should be able to:

- Understand the importance of work in people's lives.

- Understand the role and benefits of preparation in successful career planning.

- Understand the value of goal-setting as a process of career planning and selection.

- Identify mythical, stereotypical, and discriminatory ideas about work and workers.

Key Words

career:	the kind of work a person does over a period of time.
career cluster:	a group of jobs that require similar abilities and skills.
job:	the tasks or duties a person performs at the workplace.
lifestyle:	the beliefs, attitudes, and behaviour associated with a person or group; a way of life.
myth:	an opinion, belief, or ideal that has little or no basis in truth or fact.

occupation:	the work a person does to earn a living; a profession or trade.
profession:	an occupation that requires special education or training.
stereotype:	an oversimplified image of a person, group, issue, or idea; thought to be a typical example of something.
transition:	a passage from one state, condition, position, or activity to another; a process of change.
volunteer:	a person who offers services, or does something of his or her own free will, often without pay.
work:	a physical or mental activity directed toward achieving a definite goal. Also, what a person does to earn a living; a task to be done; labour; a place of employment.

Dear Gabby:

I'm seventeen years old and a senior at high school. I feel I'm constantly being bombarded with questions and decisions. What subjects am I going to take next year? Where will I go after high school? Will I continue my education? Studying what? Will I work? What kind of work do I think I'm capable of? What kind of work do I want to do? How will I support myself? Everyone I talk to is more worried about tomorrow than today.

Whatever happened to the philosophy "Live one day at a time"? These are supposed to be the best years of my life, yet it seems that planning for the future is all that anybody talks to me about. And the more questions they ask, the fewer answers I have. I feel like I'm missing out on all the fun when I get so worried about the future.

All-Worked-Up Jamie

Dear Jamie:

Living one day at a time is a good philosophy, but part of each day involves anticipating the future. It may be tomorrow's weather, next week's activities, or some long-range goal. The questions you are being asked are valid ones. You seem to sense this, too, or you would not be concerned. These are not easy questions to answer, but in this book and through a variety of resources in your school you have the opportunity to reach out for help with your studies.

When someone tells you that these are the best years of your life, they hope that you will enjoy your adolescent years, despite the transitions you undergo and the many decisions you have to make. The key to a happy life is to look forward to what each stage of life has to bring and to meet the new challenges with enthusiasm and a positive outlook. After all, wouldn't you choose to have each day better than the one before?

Today the future may seem very far away. You may not feel ready to start working or handling adult responsibilities, but this is the time you should be preparing. Think about the way you plan for a special event or a holiday. You must make decisions about where you will go, and arrange transportation, accommodation, and activities. You enjoy all the planning as you look forward to your trip. Why not look at your life the same way? It's an exciting journey, and you'll want to make the most of it every stage of the way!

Gabby Werkes

Prepare for Your Future

This book is intended to help you build your tomorrows. If you are like most people, you will spend at least thirty years in the world of work. During your lifetime you may have many jobs and several careers. Like Jamie, you may not be ready to start a full-time job, but you are in a position to begin making your future a successful and satisfying one.

As you approach graduation from high school or college, you enter a time of *transition*. Your occupation will change from that of a "student" to that of a "working person."

Every change requires adaptations and adjustments to new situations. Learning how to prepare for those changes is one of the most effective tools for dealing with each transition successfully. How will you handle your transition into the world of work? Will you be ready? What will your first and future careers be?

Choosing a career can be a difficult decision. In North America today there are thousands of careers available. Every day some of them become obsolete and new ones develop. No matter which career you choose, it will require preparation and training.

You have already begun to prepare for your future, perhaps without even knowing it. You have done this by taking courses, developing your interests and skills, and perhaps by having a part-time job or doing volunteer work. You may have a chance to gain on-the-job training in a work experience program or an in-depth co-operative education program.

This book will be a valuable resource as you prepare for your future. This chapter will help you understand more about the ideas and processes associated with work. Chapter 2 will help you get to know yourself: your abilities, your preferences, and your ideas about your future lifestyle. In later chapters, you will learn how to look for and find jobs, how to survive at the workplace, and how to cope with future transitions.

What Is Work?

Let's start with the "Key Word" definition: work is a physical or mental activity directed toward achieving a definite goal. This means different things to different people, and unfortunately work often has a bad reputation. Some people think work is boring, others see it as necessary for survival; but some love their livelihood and don't even think of it as work. Still others don't know what they would do with their time if they didn't work, and then there are those who seem to avoid it like the plague.

Think of all the meanings *work* has had for you. You may have had your first experience of work when you were asked to pick up your toys as a toddler. You watched people going to work and doing their work. You saw the garbage collector splash through the puddles that were off-limits for you; you saw construction workers operate huge cranes, you saw police officers speed down the street with their roof-top lights flashing. You saw your doctor comfort the sick, your teacher work hard all year and still have time to enjoy the summer break; and you saw members of your family doing their jobs. These impressions helped you form your notions of what work was all about.

You have done many kinds of work yourself. Your tasks and chores at home, your school work, perhaps a part-time job — all were referred to as "work" at some time or other. ("Don't you have some *work* to do?") Some work may have been pleasant for you, and some not. Even though it's a short word, "work" carries many meanings and connotations. This has always been so.

Let's look at some earlier ideas about work. The ancient Greeks believed that physical work was imposed by the gods as a punishment. They considered work to be a curse. (Do you know anyone who thinks the same way today?) There have also been cultures and times in which work was regarded as a virtue and idleness as a sin. It was (and still is) believed that hard work alone guaranteed success in life.

During the Industrial Revolution, from about 1750 to 1850, machines began to replace people in doing heavy and repetitive work. No longer was a worker's worth measured by how hard or how long one worked; rather, it was measured by the type of work one did. This period brought about a transition from "muscle power" to "brain power." It was also a time when many universities were established, and the introduction of machinery into the workplace forced many people to learn new skills. Many workers had to acquire technical training before they were considered employable.

Today, as in the past, people identify themselves by the type of work they do. But activities that are work for some people are simply enjoyable pastimes for others.

You Be the Judge: Is It Work?

As you read the following list of activities, decide whether they can be considered as "work." Classify your responses as "You bet" (always); "Maybe" (sometimes); "Hardly ever"; or "How could *that* be considered work?"

Once you have completed your notes, compare your results with those of your classmates. Discuss these comparisons in class. What have you discovered about people's ideas of work?

1. Mowing the lawn.
2. Washing the car.
3. Delivering newspapers.
4. Doing the laundry.
5. Piloting an airplane.
6. Being a flight attendant.
7. Doing a school assignment.
8. Playing hockey.
9. Playing hockey for the NHL.
10. Singing in a rock group.
11. Running for public office.
12. Being a member of the royal family.
13. Modelling new fashions.
14. Driving a truck.
15. Driving the car on a holiday.
16. Fixing a stereo.
17. Being a disc jockey.
18. Brushing your teeth.
19. Baking a cake.
20. Picking up your "toys."

Why People Work

Economic Reasons

Earnings from work enable you to purchase the basic necessities of life (food, clothing, and shelter) as well as some of your wants. Many teenagers have part-time jobs. Do you? What do you use your earnings for? Most teens use their financial rewards for "extras" such as records or tapes, clothes, and

tickets to concerts and movies. How many teens do you think establish a budget and keep careful track of their income and spending? How much money do you save from your earnings?

Having a paid job has other advantages, too. The money you earn may allow you to establish some financial independence from your family, and at the same time help you develop skills that will eventually allow you to make your own way.

Social Interaction

Just as your social circle now may include friends you made in school, working outside the home enables you to meet other people and expand that social circle. By getting to know new people and making new friends, you will find mutual interests and develop mutual activities outside work. Work also provides an opportunity for acceptance and understanding from others in a group setting.

Self-Respect

Work can develop your feelings of self-respect. A good performance and a job well done give you a sense of accomplishment. Praise from your boss or your peers builds your self-confidence.

Work Satisfaction

People who are happy with their jobs are more effective in all their activities. Usually a happy employee is also healthier than an unhappy one. If you find satisfaction in your job, you will be less likely to be late or to take days off. People who enjoy their work will likely have a happier home life. Today many people would rather have a job they enjoy than one that offers more money but less satisfaction.

Being Part of a Team

One of the basic human psychological needs is the need to "belong," to feel needed. Being part of an organization or company enables you to take pride in the group and creates that feeling of belonging. Think of the times you worked hard on a project as part of a team. How did you feel when you shared the success or the failure? Being part of a group makes successes more satisfying and failures easier to handle.

Feeling Useful, Being Active

Are you a couch potato? If you are like most people, you probably cannot sit around for too long. Working keeps you active and in touch with other people. Having a sense of purpose and direction is important for your well-being and happiness; work provides you with opportunities to be a useful member of the community.

Consider

1. "I'd go nuts if I didn't work!" Why do some people feel this way?

2. "A job gives a person a sense of identity." Explain how.

3. At a party, Bob is introduced by Susan, who says that Bob is a teacher. Bob corrects Susan by saying, "No, I *work* as a teacher." What does Bob mean?

To Do

1. Ask an acquaintance who holds a job why he or she works. Have the acquaintance do the "Is It Work?" exercise, and compare his or her answers with yours. Bring your notes back to class for sharing and discussion.

Reach

2. What happens when people don't work? Recent studies of work have examined what happens to people when they are unemployed. These studies have concluded that people depend on their jobs for their self-esteem, a sense of purpose, and opportunities for socializing. What happens to people when they don't have a job? Think about the following examples:

   ● A recently laid-off employee who has been declared redundant on the job.

   ● A person who has been unemployed for many months.

   ● A young homemaker who has decided to stay at home to care for her family.

   ● A recently retired senior citizen.

- A handicapped person who cannot persuade employers of her or his skills.

Find out, either by research at the library or by talking to people in these situations,

1. how they feel;
2. what problems they have had to face; and
3. how they have coped so far.

Volunteer Work

Most people get something in return for their work; usually it's money or satisfaction, and sometimes it's both. Many people do volunteer work, which means that they receive no money for their efforts. Workers such as "candy stripers" in hospitals, little-league baseball coaches, and people who give their time to collect charitable donations are all examples of volunteers.

Both paid workers and unpaid volunteers do productive, important work in our society. For the volunteer, however, remuneration is the sense of *giving* something to the community instead of *receiving* a paycheque.

To Do

1. In three minutes, list as many volunteer jobs as you can.
2. Compare your list with those of your classmates.
3. "An activity that is work for one person might not be work for another." Give some examples.

The Ultimate Volunteer

One of the best examples of a volunteer worker is a nun, Mother Teresa. In 1948, while teaching at a school in Calcutta, India, Mother Teresa was shocked by the suffering she

witnessed. Homeless children, lepers, and other destitute ill lay in streets and alleys, waiting to die. Mother Teresa felt compelled to leave the school and help these people.

The Roman Catholic Church granted her permission to lay aside her nun's habit and take up the blue-edged, coarse cotton sari that became the uniform of the group she founded, the Missionaries of Charity. Young women and men from all over the world joined Mother Teresa in helping the poor. They collected abandoned babies from gutters and garbage heaps and nursed them back to health. They brought in the dying so that they might die with dignity and among friends.

Missionaries working with Mother Teresa vow to give whole-hearted free service to the poorest of the poor. They cannot work for the rich; nor may they accept money for the work they do. Their main goal is to help those who need it most. Although Mother Teresa and her co-workers are not paid with money, their satisfaction comes from helping others.

Consider

1. Name some other volunteers, both well-known and not so well-known.
2. How can the experience you gain in volunteer work help your career development?
3. "The world is full of willing people. Some are willing to work, and some are willing to let them." Do you agree or disagree? Why?

Reach

4. What type of volunteer work would you like to do? Find out what kind of volunteer work is available to you, and arrange to spend a day with an organization of your choice. Report back to your class on what you did and how you felt while volunteering.

Choosing a Lifestyle

As you become an adult, you will find that you form a lifestyle of your own. Just as no two snowflakes are alike, no two people have identical lifestyles, because everyone has different values. *Values* include such abstract qualities as love, desire for success, and honesty. They play an important role in determining the goals you set out for yourself and how you choose to work toward them. If you believe that money is important, then having money becomes an important value to you. If family and friends are the most important things in your life, then you value personal relationships above everything else.

It is important to know what your values are before you make a career decision. For example, if your family is important to you and you want to spend plenty of time with them, then you may not want a career that requires a lot of travel unless it allows you to take your family along. Even if your career allows your family to travel with you, will they want to spend much time living out of a suitcase?

Goal Setting

In order to progress toward the kind of life and career you want, you must set goals for yourself. Having clear goals in mind will direct you in the choices you have to make.

To understand how important goals are, imagine you are walking along a road that stretches out to the horizon. If there were no road signs, how would you know where you were going? How would you know how far you had walked or how close you were to your destination? Goals help you find the signposts along your path in life.

Have you thought about your goals? What do you want to accomplish? What do you want to do with your life? What sort of life do you want?

If you want to be happy in your career, one of the first things you need to do is develop a plan. A good plan has an attainable goal and outlines the steps you have to take to reach that goal. In order to set that goal, you must know yourself. The exercises in Chapter 2 will help you to do just that. Later, Chapter 10 will help you to recognize milestones in your life and assist you in making a plan.

Unfortunately, some students end up in careers for which they are ill-suited. Often this occurs because they do not know what they really want out of life. They may choose courses because they like the teacher, or they want to be with their friends, or they think a course will be easy. They don't realize that the decisions they make now can have a great impact on their future.

The career decisions you make with a goal in mind are more likely to lead you to success. In fact, as you come closer to your goal, feelings of satisfaction will already begin and motivate you to keep working. Let's take a look at how this works.

To Do

1. Imagine that your career goal is to be a doctor. In a group or as a class, discuss the answers you would give to the following questions.
   - What would you need to know about:
     — your physical abilities and limitations?
     — your values?
     — your mental abilities?
     — your desired lifestyle?
     — your chosen career?
   - Outline the step-by-step plan you might make to achieve your goal. The plan could consist of short-range goals leading toward your main long-range goal.
   - What are some of the difficulties you might have to confront along the way, and what decisions will you have to make?
2. Try the preceding exercise with your own career goal in mind. Don't be afraid to dream a little; set your sights high. With hard work and determination, you may surprise yourself and achieve your goal.
3. How attainable is your career goal? To answer this question, you will need more information. List all the career information resources available at your school. Where else might you look for more information?
4. Choose a career cluster that interests you, and visit your school's guidance department to find more information about it. List all the possible jobs in your career cluster. Highlight the ones that interest you, and then list the things that attract you to these careers.

Does the career cluster you chose include careers you are not familiar with? Find out more about these careers.

5. To help you focus on your career goal, it's useful to know what you want from work. Describe your ideal career — the kind of work you would like to do. What advantages does it have? Use the following list to put the advantages of your ideal career into three categories:

    Very Important,
    Somewhat Important, or
    Not Important.

    If some of the advantages of your ideal career are not included in the following list, add them to your own list.

    I would like a job that:
    ● pays a lot of money.
    ● is not boring.
    ● gives me a lot of authority.
    ● enables me to dress up.
    ● makes my parents proud of me.
    ● has a lot of holidays.
    ● has a lot of security.
    ● has a lot of responsibility.
    ● people regard as a "status" job.
    ● provides an opportunity to travel.
    ● enables me to meet new people.
    ● provides me with new experiences.
    ● enables me to continue my education.
    ● encourages me to invent new products or develop new ideas.
    ● makes me think for myself.
    ● gives me a feeling of accomplishment.
    ● allows me to help those in need.
    ● I enjoy doing.

Look over your list of "Very Important" advantages. Does your ideal career have all these advantages? It should. Later you will find out what qualifications the career requires of you. Keep an open mind and be flexible when doing your career research. It will be important to keep both a career's advantages and its demands in mind as you develop a career plan.

At this point, you may want to share your findings with someone who is "in the know." You may discover that your ideal career is one you had not considered before. It may not exist exactly as you wish, and you may have to make some compromises. It's also worth remembering that your ideal career may not be the only career you have in your lifetime.

Keeping an Open Mind

Myths About Work

Have you ever heard any of the following statements, or similar ones?

- "Boys become doctors, girls become nurses."

- "I'll make more money if I go to university."

- "Why can't I drop math? I don't need it to become a hairdresser."

- "Why should I worry about planning a career? All I need is a job until I stop working to raise a family."

- "Why do I have to take these aptitude tests? I know what I can do."

- "I only know how to do *this* job. What will happen to me when I'm replaced by a computer?"

- "Lots of people don't like their jobs."

- "If I don't like my job, I'll just quit. There's always unemployment insurance or welfare."

- "You'd better make the right career choice now—you won't be able to change it later!"

- "Learning stops when you leave school."

Each of these statements represents a mythical, stereotypical, or discriminatory idea about work or workers. None of them has any place in today's progressive society. Beware of such ideas; they limit people. Let's take a closer look at some of these issues.

Today, whether you are a woman or a man, you are encouraged to pursue any career you want. Your choice should not be limited by sex-role stereotypes. All employers know that it is illegal to favour either sex for a particular job. Smart employers know that it makes good business sense to hire the most capable person for a position, regardless of the person's sex.

Education is a good way to increase your earning power, but it does not determine it. Today many workers in the skilled trades earn more than teachers or accountants who have several years of university training. Education provides you with the qualifications for the career you wish to pursue.

A well-rounded education will make you a more flexible and marketable employee. A certain subject in school may not seem necessary for the career you are planning, but the more basic skills you have the greater your chances will be in any career. Your chances for advancement will also be better.

Planning to have a family should not keep you from having a career. Child-care responsibilities can be shared by both parents and supplemented by day-care arrangements. Staying home to raise your children may be either a long-range career choice or simply a stage in your life. Many employers will arrange temporary leaves of absence or part-time work for valued employees. Financial considerations may require both parents to work. Why not work at the career of your choice?

Examine your skills and capabilities carefully, and ask for the opinions of others. Do you have abilities that you are unaware of, but that others see clearly? Many employment agencies and high school guidance offices offer aptitude tests that may help you discover your hidden strengths.

Computers frighten and intimidate many people, but remember that a computer is only a tool. It is used by people to make them more effective workers. Get friendly with computers. For those who choose not to work with computers, there will always be jobs that can only be performed by a person.

Being happy in your job will affect many other areas of your life. Liking your work will certainly make it more pleasant to wake up in the morning. However, don't expect to enjoy every aspect of your work. The part you focus on will affect your attitude toward all of your work. If you discover that you really dislike a great deal of your job's duties, you should consider a change.

We are fortunate in Canada to have the benefit of government assistance when we are out of work. Leaving your job because you do not like it is a legitimate reason to apply for government benefits, but unless you actively try to find another job you may find that you are no longer eligible for assistance.

Making the "right" career choice now is certainly the ideal; however, in the future the average person may actually have several careers. As new jobs are created, you may seek a change. As some older jobs become redundant, it may be necessary to retrain for a new or different kind of work.

No matter what you do in your search for a fulfilling career, strive to learn something new each day. The new things you learn will make you a more interesting person and a more valuable employee.

Many books have been written about the world of work. It is an exciting and dynamic place, always changing and always presenting something new for you to learn. To find your place in it, you will want to know as much about yourself and your career interests as possible. And that's what Chapter 2 is all about!

Career Development

After completing this chapter, you should be able to:

- Identify your strengths, weaknesses, and interests, and relate them to the careers and jobs that you wish to explore.

- Identify some of your transferable skills.

- Identify several sources of career and job information.

- Explore these sources for information about job availability and requirements such as training, qualifications, entry-level positions, and potential for advancement.

- Develop a list of possible jobs in your career area of interest.

Key Words

ability: the power to do something, either mental or physical.

aptitude: a natural ability or talent in any area, such as technology, communication, art, music, science, or athletics.

attitude: a certain disposition, perspective, or belief that affects a person's behaviour.

career development:	self-development through the study and integration of a person's interests, abilities, aspirations, values, and circumstances.
career planning:	the decision-making process by which a person identifies possible career options and the steps required to have a certain career.
interests:	the personal likes and dislikes that affect the choices a person makes.
life skills:	skills that enable a person to cope with the stresses and challenges of life; for example, communication skills, decision-making skills, resource and time-management skills, and planning skills.
personality traits:	the qualities and characteristics that shape a person's unique character and identity.
skill:	the ability to do something as a result of training, practice, or knowledge.
transferable skills:	skills that can be used in a variety of jobs or occupations.
temperament:	a quality of personality that shows up in the way a person thinks, acts, or responds to people or situations.

Getting to Know Yourself

You are about to begin a very exciting journey. It is the journey of your own career development. But before you set out to develop any kind of plan, you must know where you are starting from. Knowing yourself will help you to set goals for the future and make plans to achieve them.

In Chapter 1 you looked at ideas about work and the possible kinds of work that might interest you. In this chapter, you will have a chance to look closely at the one who will be working — you!

How Well Do You Know Yourself?

Dear Gabby:

I'm a senior in high school. Like most seniors, I'm trying to figure out what subjects I should be taking and what to do after I graduate. It seems that everyone I talk to knows better than I do what I should do. I have many interests, especially in the creative design field, and I'm also really good at math and science. I love taking languages, and I don't want to give up my study of these, either.

When someone asks me what career I would like to pursue, I don't know what to say. I could tell them the things I would like to do, or I can tell them about what everyone else thinks I should do. For example, I think I could be very good at interior design or carpentry. I really enjoy working with wood and have made my own furniture. I used to work part-time in a hair salon. This is something I love doing. I really enjoy the "people" part of it, making them look attractive and feel good about themselves.

My parents say that I should try for a more professional and prestigious job, since my marks are good. They suggest I go into law or engineering. My language teacher says I could easily become an international interpreter. This sounds interesting, but I'm not sure that I want to be interpreting what other people are saying all the time; I have so many of my own ideas. My friends are encouraging me to open my own design studio, but I don't know the first thing about running my own business. My guidance counsellor thinks I should go to university and keep my options open. This makes me feel as if I am not really going anywhere.

I'm getting more confused by the minute. Do you have any advice?

Confused Calvin in Calgary

Dear Calvin:
Yours is not an uncommon problem; in fact, this book is a

response to requests such as yours. It sounds as if your forces are scattered now. I would suggest you try to do a personal inventory of your abilities, skills, and interests, and also consider the kind of lifestyle you wish to have in the future. This will include examining your personality and temperament.

There are a number of self-tests you can do. You should also do some of your own investigation: What are the jobs you have mentioned really like? Talk to people who do these jobs. Find out what the jobs' demands are. Do these people have the kind of lifestyles you would like to have? Keep reading. Your problem is what this chapter is all about!

Gabby Werkes

Since you will probably work about eighty thousand hours in your lifetime, it's worth giving a great deal of thought to getting to know yourself before you choose a career. Getting to know yourself can be an exciting and rewarding exercise. It is something you should do regularly as you continue to change and grow. Businesses do this to know where they stand. Periodically, throughout the year, a store or a company takes stock, or an inventory, of its goods and accounts to make sure that the business is in good health. Based on the information it gathers, decisions can be made more wisely and with prospects of greater success.

Taking an inventory of yourself will help you to know yourself better and give you a basis for exploring the many career and lifestyle options available to you.

To Do — Personal Inventory

Part 1
Do this part alone on a separate sheet of paper.

Introduce yourself as you would in person, and describe yourself and your life so far by completing the following exercise.

Self-Image

Give reasons for each statement. For example,"I am . . . because. . . ." Don't be afraid to boast a little here; emphasize your strong points.

1. I can best be described by these three words:
2. I have chosen these words because:
3. I like to spend my time:
4. I am good at (list at least five things):
5. I am happiest when:
6. My major interests are:
7. Three accomplishments I am proud of are:
8. Three things I find difficult are:
9. I often worry about:
10. The beliefs that are very important to me are:

Background

1. My family background is:
2. I have lived in these places:
3. Three significant events in my life are:
4. They made me feel:

Education

1. My best subject is:
2. My favourite subject is . . . because:
3. My worst subject is:
4. My most significant accomplishment at school is... and it made me feel:
5. My learning skills are (excellent, good, fair, varied):
6. My feelings about education are:
7. My present educational goal is:
8. My future educational goal is:

Work Experience

1. Describe your experience in the world of work, including jobs you have held, either paid or volunteer, and school-related work experience such as co-operative education.
2. For each of the work experiences you described, briefly outline what you liked and/or disliked about each one, what skills you used/learned, whether

you would consider this area of work for your future career, and, of course, why.

3. What kind of work would you like to do?
4. What do your family, teachers, and close friends suggest you consider as a career option? How do you feel about their suggestions?
5. List all the career options that you would be interested in exploring.
6. Describe any fears you have about the prospects of employment.

Personal and Recreational Interests

1. In my spare time, I like to:

2. The skills required for these activities are:

3. In the future, I would like to . . . because:

4. I haven't done this yet because:

Part 2
Do this part with others.

In the second part of this inventory-taking exercise, share your inventory with someone else. You will receive that person's inventory in return. After reading someone else's inventory, prepare a brief statement that tells what you have learned about that person, what goals or interests you share, or what you find interesting about that person. Then give him or her some clues about career areas that you think may be appropriate. For example, "You're good at ____, like doing ____, and are interested in ____. Have you thought about __(list careers, jobs, etc.)?"

If you are ambitious, this is an exercise you can do with the whole class to multiply the feedback you receive. You still share your personal inventory with another person. But then, based on your inventory, that person shares with the class by introducing you and telling a bit about you. You do the same for that person. The class may respond on a ballot, which is then given to you, or it can respond orally if there is enough time available.

Consider

From doing these exercises,
1.   I have learned that I:
2.   I discovered that others:
3.   I was surprised by:
4.   I'm going to give some more thought to:

You Be the Judge

Suppose that you have a particular career interest in an area in which you possess exceptional talent and potential. It will require you to obtain considerable postsecondary education and training. Your family is very supportive of you. Your teachers and counsellor at school feel you will be very successful if you develop your aptitudes into abilities. This will involve a considerable amount of money and time.

Despite their enthusiasm, your parents cannot help you financially. Your boyfriend or girlfriend is getting serious about your relationship and wants to marry you after you graduate. This will mean going to work instead of continuing your education. What will you do? Why?

The YOU Collage

A helpful technique in meeting goals is to visualize what you are aiming for. The following activity involves this, as well as illustrating who you are now. Using pictures, symbols, and key words, you are going to piece together a jigsaw that illustrates your many aspects. In art, this is called a collage.

Try to represent something about your interests, hobbies, relationships with others, values, personality, lifestyle, and career goals. Prepare your collage at home and bring it to class without letting anyone know it is yours.

Here's what you will need:
- A mounting board. Choose a colour that says something about you.
- Some old magazines. Use their pictures and graphic symbols and words from their headlines.
- Scissors, glue, paints, and markers.

In Class

1. Pass around the unidentified collages. Your teacher will then take them one at a time and let the class discuss them and guess who they belong to. Any guess must be accompanied by reasons for that match. The discussion about each collage should include some interesting things people see about the person you have portrayed.

2. Once all the collages have been discussed, each person should explain his or her own collage. You might want to ask the class about the comments that were made about yours. This will help you to understand how others see you.

3. Now that you have heard your classmates' opinions, answer the following questions.
   - Which comments about the collage verified what you wanted to show about yourself?
   - Which comments surprised you? Why? How do they make you feel? Do you feel they are accurate?
   - Which of your characteristics revealed in your collage would you like to improve or change?
   - What changes, if any, would you make to your collage so that it would portray you more accurately?

The preparation you do now in getting to know yourself will help you to select the career and lifestyle that will fit you best. It is a wise investment in your future happiness and success. Here are some additional points for you to consider.

Your Goals and Dreams

Dream a little; it will give you important clues to the lifestyle you are aiming for. But don't expect simply to "fall into" your future work. Why not find the career that will fit into your dreams and fulfil them? Your career so often determines your lifestyle. Make sure it is the one you want to live with.

Your Interests

Think about the things you enjoy doing the most. These are probably things that you do well and that bring you satisfaction and a sense of excitement.

How do you enjoy spending your spare time now? Do you often wish you had more time to do the things you enjoy? Find out what career areas may match those kinds of activities. For example, do you enjoy

- helping others?
- getting others to do their best?
- being part of a team?
- physical activity?
- mechanical things?
- talking?
- working alone?

Remember that the more interests you have now, the greater will be your chances of finding a satisfying career.

Case

You may find that you can combine several interests in one career. Patrick, for example, has always had a mechanical flair. He enjoys creating new machines and fixing ones that don't work. Patrick also is really happy when he can be helpful to others. He is good with people of all ages and backgrounds. In fact, working with the public is high on Patrick's list of priorities for his future career.

To Do

Suggest five careers that Patrick should consider.

Your Career Activity Preference

Your present interests may help you determine your preferred career activity. Are you interested in people, data, or things? You may be interested in a combination of them. If so, consider these options:

- If you enjoy people *and* data, then perhaps you may want to work in travel, or education, or business, or sales.

- If you prefer to work alone with things *and* data, then perhaps drafting, or computer operations, or lab technology may be for you.

- If you enjoy contact with people *and* like working with things, then consider the medical professions, or personal services such as hairstyling, or work in hotels and restaurants.

Just having an interest in a career is not all that is necessary to be successful in it. Consider also your aptitudes and skills.

Your Aptitudes and Skills

Another way to find out what career you may enjoy is to consider your aptitudes. Aptitudes are those mental and physical abilities that are most natural for you.

Here are some common aptitudes and the careers you might associate with them:

- ability with numbers: an accountant or mathematician

- manual dexterity: a painter or mechanic

- ability to use words well: a writer or editor

- ability to work well with children: a teacher or nurse

- creativity: an actor, dancer, or artist

What are your aptitudes? What do others tell you about what you seem to be talented at? Ask for their opinions.

Skills are those aptitudes that you have developed. Knowing what your aptitudes are is the first step in developing a skill. For example, not all students who have aptitudes in certain subjects in school develop them into skills. It does take effort and a desire to improve yourself. A part of this effort must go into your academic training.

Your Academic Abilities

It is important to realize your academic potential so that you will be able to enrol in the courses that will lead you to an area of success. Doing well in school now will also help you develop skills that ensure success in the future: self-discipline, perseverance, and dedication to your work. You should review the areas you have aptitude in with your counsellors, who will also tell you about the requirements for graduation, apprenticeship training, or postsecondary education.

Your Values and Moral Beliefs

As a youngster you learned from your family the things that were considered important for living well. You are now at the age where you are developing your own views about what is important in your life and what is necessary for a successful and happy life. You may keep some of your family's values and add some new ones of your own. Whatever you decide, you will question the importance of certain values, and your answers will have an effect on the kind of career you choose.

To Do

Consider some of these values. Which ones are important to you?

- Having lots of friends.
- Being healthy.
- Having a happy home life.
- Being creative.
- Being helpful to others.
- Having a powerful position.
- Having an active role in your religion.
- Earning a lot of money.

What other values are important to you? How would they affect the career you choose?

Your Physical Make-up and Health

Have you considered the physical stamina and health that a certain job may demand of you? Every job makes some demands on your body and mind. Does the job require standing, lifting, a high degree of hand–eye co-ordination, good eyesight, or long periods of high concentration? Knowing the physical requirements of a job before you begin will ensure that you preserve your health.

Your Temperament

Temperament refers to your emotional make-up. This is an important consideration in preparation for your career. If your temperament is one of little patience, you would probably not want to consider being a cashier, flight attendant, or doctor. However, if patience is one of your strong qualities, then teaching, sales, and the medical profession are areas for you to explore.

There are many areas of personality that you will want to be aware of when choosing a career, and there are many personality tests on the market. Your guidance centre or a job-placement office will be of great assistance here. It will be able to recommend some tests to you, arrange for you to do them, and help you with analysing them.

To Do

There are aspects of your personality that you can develop. Consider the personality aspects listed below and discuss, with your group or class, why they are desirable traits in an employee.
- a positive attitude
- common sense
- courtesy
- dependability
- enthusiasm
- a desire to succeed
- foresight

Once you have discussed these traits in class, write down how you would describe yourself now with respect to each of these. What are your strengths? What areas need improvement? What can you do to improve them?

Where Can You Find Out About Careers?

You have done a considerable amount of self-discovery in this chapter. This is a very important part of your career exploration. But in order to find the "right" job, you also need to obtain information about what the jobs are like. There are at least seven thousand different occupations in Canada today. How do you find out which kinds of jobs are available? Where do you find out about occupations that interest you? Fortunately, there are many sources of information.

Career Information Centres

Never before in history has there been as much information about careers and occupations as there is now. This makes your research much easier. The more sources you contact and make use of, the more accurate your information will be.

Specialized career information centres, sponsored by the federal and provincial governments, are very helpful. Their information is available in several forms:

- pamphlets and booklets about careers and postsecondary institutions and their requirements.

- career resource directories such as:

    —*Canadian Classification and Dictionary of Occupations* (CCDO) and "Careers Canada" series from Employment and Immigration Canada.
    —"Choices," an interactive, computerized career information system.

- occupational monographs published by provincial ministries of colleges and universities.

- books about specific careers.

- films or videos that provide an audiovisual representation of a career as well as information about it.

At Your School

Guidance Offices

As well as providing assistance in course selection and aptitude testing, your school's guidance office may offer programs such as "Choices" or S.G.I.S. (Student Guidance Information System). Both these computer/video information programs offer plenty of information about careers. Your counsellor may be able to suggest people in your community or former graduates of your school with whom you could discuss career options.

Courses

If your school offers a career development course, be sure to select it as one of your options. Your school may have other resources that show career clusters (groups of similar careers), the qualifications required, and the institutions that offer accredited courses for your career choices.

Libraries

Most libraries have a career information section. This may include vertical files, microfiche, videos, and books about various careers and people who are involved in certain kinds of work.

Postsecondary Institutions

Most postsecondary institutions such as colleges and universities have placement centres. These centres are intended to assist graduates in finding work. Don't be afraid to walk into one and introduce yourself as a potential student. As long as they are not too busy, the placement counsellors can give you some significant insights into the potential job market. The centres may offer other services such as a career-information and job board. Take a look at the kinds of jobs that are being offered to graduates of such institutions. Would they interest you?

Investigative Interviews

Meet with a person who is successful in the career you're interested in. You should go to the interview prepared to ask significant questions about the occupation and what it involves. You will find a list of suggested questions on pages 39–40. The interview should take place in the area where the person is working so that you can decide whether this is the type of environment in which you would like to work. Ask the person to show you the kinds of work he or she does. Find out about the potential opportunities in that line of work. Ask about anything that may concern you!

Don't forget to speak to family members, friends, and neighbours about their careers, or ask for their suggestions for further investigation.

On-the-Job Experience

Once you have done the investigative work suggested above, you probably will have narrowed your selections. You might want to try a hands-on experience in a work area that interests you. Work-experience programs have many different forms and are called by various names. Find out whether your school offers such an opportunity, what it involves, and what it will require from you.

You may very well already be enrolled in such a program. Congratulations! You not only have the valuable opportunity of finding out about the career and its future, but you are already making important contacts for your future job placement. Employers who already know of someone with a good work reputation don't need to advertise positions.

If no such programs are available to you, consider part-time or summer employment in your area of interest. Volunteer work too can provide valuable insights into what a career is really like. You will develop some useful skills along the way if you are a resourceful person, and you will gain a sense of responsibility and self-confidence.

Where Do You Fit In?

Do you feel you have a fairly good understanding of yourself? Remember that, as time goes on, you evolve and change, and the inventory you take now may change in a year or several years' time. But if you have been thorough in your self-inventory, you are ready to start matching what you know about yourself to the careers you have investigated. Again, there are many sources to help you do this, and the more of them you pursue, the more information you will have to make a wise choice.

Your school or career centre will be helpful here. Go back to the sources of career information and review the personality traits necessary for the career list you now have. Is your personality compatible with the careers that interest you? Following is a list of questions you will want to ask yourself as you try to match your personality and career choice.

- Does this career suit your interests and activities?

- Does it fit in with your values?

- Do you have the aptitudes to develop the necessary skills?

- Does this career satisfy the way you like and need to work (with data, things, and/or people)?

- Are the salary and benefits sufficient to meet the lifestyle you wish to achieve? (Remember that entry-level positions pay considerably less. Have you looked at the long term?)

- Will you be able to meet the educational requirements for this job?

- Is there anything about this career that will make it a poor choice?

- Is there or will there be a *need* for this type of work?

Although you may change your mind later, your present career choice is a goal for you to work toward. It will provide a focus for all your actions and decisions. Just as your career will determine your lifestyle in the years to come, your choices now will lead you along a path to your career goal. In order to achieve those goals and to "fit in," sacrifices and compromises will sometimes be necessary. Keep your goal foremost in your mind, and ultimately you will achieve it and live it.

Now, let's move on to find out how to let the world know about the qualified person you are. How can you become the most desirable candidate?

The World Of Work

CHAPTER 3

Preparing for the World of Work

After completing this chapter, you should be able to:

- Identify an employer's expectations of you.
- Identify and evaluate your expectations of work.
- Find a job vacancy.
- Prepare an effective résumé.
- Complete an application form properly.
- Prepare effectively for an interview.
- Conduct yourself appropriately during an interview.
- Evaluate and follow up on your interview.

Key Words

applicant: a person who applies for a position; a job-seeker requesting employment with a company.

application form: a standardized form intended to be completed by a job applicant to provide routine background information about the applicant. Usually companies and institutions prepare these forms to focus on their specific requirements.

entry level:	the starting position upon beginning employment; often a training position.
evaluation:	the measurement of progress toward the achievement of specific goals and objectives; a judgement about the quality and/or quantity of these goals.
expectations:	beliefs or hopes about an event or outcome in the future.
interview:	a meeting of two or more people for the purpose of obtaining information about an applicant's aptitude, skills, and suitability.
interviewer:	a person who selects prospective employees through an interview.
letter of application:	a letter written to secure an interview with a prospective employer by attracting attention to the applicant's suitability. It usually accompanies a résumé, and is also known as a covering letter.
monitor:	to supervise and keep records of objectives and the progress toward those objectives.
personal image:	the qualities communicated to others by a person's appearance and behaviour.
résumé:	a summary of career and qualifications prepared by an applicant seeking a job position. Also known as a work autobiography or curriculum vitae.
self-image:	what a person thinks of himself or herself.

What Does an Employer Expect from You?

Your Character

Dear Kid:

Today you asked me for a job. From the look of your shoulders as you walked out the door, I suspect you've been turned down before, and maybe you believe by now that kids out of high school can't find work.

But I *did* hire a teenager today. You saw him. He was the one with the polished shoes and necktie. What was so special about him? Not experience; neither of you had any. It was his attitude that put him on the payroll instead of you. Attitude, son, *attitude*. He wanted that job badly enough to shuck the leather jacket, get a haircut, and look in the phone book to find out what this company makes. He did his best to impress me. That's where he edged you out.

You see, Kid, the people who hire people aren't "with" a lot of things. We have some Stone Age ideas about who owes whom a living. Maybe that makes us prehistoric, but there's nothing wrong with the cheques we sign, and if you want one, you'd better tune into our wavelength.

Ever hear of "empathy"? It's the trick of seeing the other person's side of things. I couldn't have cared less that you're behind in your car payments. That's your problem. What I needed was someone who'd go into the plant, keep his eyes open, and work for me like he'd work for himself. If you have even the vaguest idea of what I'm trying to say, let it show the next time you ask for a job. You'll be head and shoulders above the rest.

You may not believe it, but all around you employers are looking for young men and women smart enough to go after a job in the old-fashioned way. When they find one, they can't wait to unload some of their worries on their new employee.

For both our sakes, get eager, will you?

"The Boss"
(Author unknown)

Do You Have What It Takes?

There are character traits that are common to all good employees, no matter what their job happens to be. Employers will look for these traits in job applicants. Use the following rating system for each item in the list to assess your desirability as an employee: excellent (E), good (G), average (A), below average (B), or unsure (U).

Character traits

Honesty
Punctuality
Intelligence
Enthusiasm for work
Health
~Conscientiousness
Responsibility
Self-motivation
Willingness to follow directions
~Initiative
Self-confidence
Leadership
Ability to get along with others
Ability to handle conflict
Job-related skills
- Aptitudes
Social skills
Communication skills
Maturity
Emotional stability

Consider

1. Look over the completed list and compare your areas of strength (E, G, and A) and weakness (B and U). The areas of strength will be those qualities you will want to feature and have an employer take note of. Areas of weakness need attention to become strengths.

2. When you consider your weaknesses, list them, and for each one suggest a plan consisting of the steps

needed to make an improvement. Start making those improvements *today* so that they will become a real and natural part of you.

3.   Share your list of positive and improvable traits with someone else. Ask if he or she would have rated you in the same way. By doing this you are checking the accuracy of your self-image against the image you convey to others. How do the two images compare? What have you learned about yourself by doing this exercise?

Marketing Yourself

In addition to being aware of your character traits, you need to know how to market yourself. Only ten out of every one hundred applicants actually get an interview. How will you make potential employers aware of the fine employee you could be?

Usually you market yourself in two ways: your *documentation*, that is, your application form, résumé, and letter of application; and your *self-presentation*, which will most likely occur during an interview. A great deal depends on your written documentation. It will be your advertisement, and it should impress an employer enough to give you an interview.

Employers use the applicants' written documentation to screen applicants. Will yours go onto the pile of applicants to contact or into the wastepaper basket? The time and care you invest here will have significant pay-offs and may determine your future. We will examine this more closely in a later section of this book.

What Will Work Really Be Like?

Many of you have had considerable work experience before reading this book. Some of you have had part-time jobs or volunteer positions, some of you may be co-operative education students, and others may have had other school-related work experience. While you were on the job you learned what it's like to start work, what it's like to have too much work or not enough work, and what it's like to get that first paycheque.

To Do

1. In class, discuss some of the memorable work experiences you have had.

2. After the discussion, have some fun and create a list of "Little-known Facts about the World of Work." If you have had some work experience, you can rely on that to be your resource. If you have not had any real work experience, try to imagine what it must be like. When you are done, compare your ideas with those of the group having experience. How do your views differ?

Dear Gabby:

I'm a co-op student working for the summer. I have a job placement that I was really looking forward to. I work in the accessories department of a large and very prestigious store. In the future I plan to attend college to study fashion merchandising. My marks in school are quite good, and I average in the high seventies and low eighties.

Why am I telling you all this? I want you to know that I am a serious person who hopes to be a manager someday in such a store. So what's my problem? Actually, there are a couple of complaints I have, and I just don't know how to go about improving the situation.

I don't think I'm taken seriously by my supervisor. I always get the clean-up jobs. I specialize in "Windexing" the counter tops and showcases. I spend almost an hour every day just doing that! I didn't come here to be someone's maid! When new stock comes in, I'm the one who always gets to put it out on the floor. This means doing a lot of paperwork to check that every belt and purse and pair of socks is counted and priced and that the prices are correct. Isn't this someone else's responsibility? Why do I seem to get all the dirty jobs?

And if some of the other employees need something — for example, change from the cash office — they come and ask my supervisor if they can "borrow" me! Meanwhile, I have to leave behind what I am doing to run their errands, and I get so behind in my work that I have to hurry and finish before I leave.

One day I had so many of these errands I didn't even get a chance to get started on the list of tasks my supervisor had left me to do. When she came in the next day, she said she was disappointed that I didn't get any work done the day before and that she thought I was more responsible and capable of working on my own. I *am*, when I get the chance.

I don't want to sound negative. I really like the accessories department, but there is something wrong. I didn't think work would be so full of hassles. Do you think I should change jobs?

Retail Cinderella

To Do

1. Do you think Cinderella has a valid complaint? Before you read Gabby's answer, write down the advice you would give Retail Cinderella.

2. After you have written your reply, share it with someone else. How do your responses compare? Now

read Gabby's answer. How does your response compare with hers?

Dear Cindy:

I think you will agree that changing jobs would be running away from the situation and from something you say you like. Let's look at some of the problems you seem to be having.

Keeping a workplace clean, neat, and attractive is a very important part of the merchandising of products. Besides, every job has its maintenance tasks. Take a look around at other departments and other employees. What kind of housekeeping chores must they do? Often, entry-level employees get to do these tasks. It's sort of a test. Instead of complaining, do your best at it. It's one job that will have very visible results. And remember that the way you carry out these tasks and the attitude you convey will create an impression on your employer about how you will take on other, more challenging, responsibilities. If you cannot do the simple tasks well and take pride in your work, why should an employer believe you would do any better on the big jobs?

It sounds like the store has already given you considerable responsibility. Receiving and putting out stock is a very important part of retailing. This is a task that requires great accuracy; the store depends on you to report any errors. Its profits depend on this, and when you are an employee your pay and the existence of your job depend on the store's profits. Do you really want such responsibility? Do you think you can handle it?

Being a "gofer" and running errands is another of the beginner's blessings. Perhaps the store is trying to give you a break from what you are doing. It's true that too many of these breaks can prevent you from doing your assigned tasks and can lead to your supervisor wondering about the work you are accomplishing. When you are misunderstood that way, you must practise some honesty and assertiveness. Your supervisor may need to be reminded of the many interruptions you have had. Plan what you will say so that you do not sound negative and whiny; voice a conscientious concern, yet a willingness to help with whatever you can.

It really comes down to attitude and perspective. You may need to look at things in a more positive way or look at your tasks as opportunities to grow. It will take your best and constant effort, but you will find that you enjoy your work much more.

Stay *positive*!

Gabby Werkes

Consider

Full-time work can be quite different from a part-time job. As you read the following letter, note some of the surprises Michael has. Have you had a similar experience?

Dear Gabby:

For as long as I can remember, I've always wanted to be a photographer. I'm really good at it, and I work for a really great company. I have always looked forward to "growing up and being free." But I've been working for several months now, and I'm finding that being grown-up is not all it's cracked up to be and I'm not all that free. I had always hoped that when I started working full-time and no longer had homework at night, I would be able to go out more and see more of my friends. Just the opposite is true! I don't get home until 7 p.m., and by the time I have dinner and clean up, it's getting pretty late. I'm almost ashamed to say that I feel too tired to go out by that time.

I did go out one night, and the next morning I almost slept in, I didn't have my lunch ready, and I felt like a disaster area the whole day. To make matters worse, my friends have nicknamed me "the Monk," because they hardly ever see me.

Am I doing something wrong? Maybe I'm not ready for this "freedom"?

Mike the Monk

Dear Mike:

The situation you describe is not unusual at all. Many of us have had to adjust to full-time work. You do have a long day at work. It's a considerably different schedule from the one you kept as a student. Not only does that mean a lifestyle change, but it also requires time for your body to adjust.

I'm delighted to hear that you are so pleased with the work you do, because that will make your readjustment that much easier. As for your friends, try to see them on weekends. Perhaps you will be able to share some of your experience with them and help them to prepare a little more realistically for their transition to work.

Now, about the freedom you feel you are missing: the reality of freedom is that it carries responsibilities with it. You sound like a responsible fellow. I am sure that eventually you will understand that our youthful idea of freedom, and the reality of freedom, responsibility, and the satisfaction of achieving independence, are quite different things and bring quite different satisfactions in one's life.

In the meantime, as you adjust to your new-found adult responsibilities, don't forget to plan and enjoy your weekends.

Gabby Werkes

Where Should You Look for Job Vacancies?

Part of the challenge in your career research was exploring the job market and investigating the availability of positions in your career interest area. Finding an actual job opening and an employer interested in your skills and abilities is your next task.

To Do

1. In class, discuss the ways in which you and your classmates obtained your part-time jobs. Examine the following three aspects of the job search:

   - How you discovered that a job was available.
   - The steps you went through before being hired.
   - Why you think you, rather than other applicants, got the job.

2. Why do job vacancies occur? List five reasons.

3. How many ways are there of learning about job vacancies? List as many as you can.

Taking the Initiative

It has been estimated that, every day in Canada, as many as ten thousand jobs become vacant! More than half of the vacancies are never advertised. Whenever a worker retires, is promoted, resigns, or is fired, a position is created. Could it be one for you? How will you let employers know that you want to work for them, if and when an opportunity arises? Why not pick the employers you would like to work for and let them know you're available? This is one of the most successful job-search techniques.

Even if there is no job available at the time you apply, you may be called upon later when an opening does arise. Some employers, anticipating their future needs, hire applicants who show exceptional potential and create a job for them.

You can find the names of potential employers in the yellow pages, in a newspaper's sales and service advertisements, and in business directories, which are available at a public library or from the business taxation department at city hall.

Personal contacts can help in your job hunt. When friends, relatives, neighbours, and teachers know that you are looking for work, they can provide you with leads. Your previous part-time employers may also have business contacts for you. They may even want to hire you in a full-time capacity themselves!

Consider

"It's not *what* you know, but *who* you know, that counts." Have you heard this before? It's partly true and partly false. Think of circumstances in which this may be true, and to what extent it's true. What are the limitations of this idea?

Responding to Advertised Opportunities

Many employers advertise their available positions. Check the classified ads in newspapers. Some newspapers have special "careers" sections in addition to the "want" ads. Be selective in responding to the ads; most reputable employers will include their name and information on how to contact them.

Canada Employment Centres are good places to find out about available positions. Private employment agencies also offer services to put you in touch with employers; employers use these agencies to advertise their needs to those who are job-hunting. Such agencies can help both you and the employer; since the needs of both parties are known, they are more effectively matched.

Have you considered making "cold calls"? Cold calling is much like canvassing; even though a job opening has not been advertised, you telephone or make a personal visit to a potential employer to ask for work.

To Do

1. Why might making a cold call be a little scary? Describe how you would feel making such a call.

2. What could you do to create a positive impression? What skills would be useful?

3. What does the simple fact of you making a cold call tell a potential employer about you?

Reach

4. Role playing: With a partner, prepare to make a cold call. One of you will act as the employer, the other as the applicant. Let the class judge whether you have been successful or not. Ask your classmates how they would have responded if they were the employer. Include constructive criticism in your discussion.

If you have participated in a co-operative education or work experience program, you already have your foot in the employer's door. These learning opportunities often blossom into permanent employment. Employers particularly favour people like you because they have already received considerable training and have already shown what kind of workers they will be.

Remember to keep these sources of job information in mind:

● the school guidance or placement office

- professional and trade journals
- government departments and agencies
- union offices
- the "hidden" job market

The Hidden Job Market

The hidden job market refers to unusual job opportunities that people seldom consider. Read the following case to see how Soria may land her job.

Case

Soria had recently graduated from high school, where she completed a business program. All through school she had made extra money by babysitting for Mrs. Lloyd. Her typing skills were fair, but she was not thrilled at the prospect of being a secretary and sitting at a desk for the better part of the day; nor did she really relish the idea of going on to college. Even if she were to choose college, she had no idea what she would study.

Summer holidays were already under way, and Soria was becoming concerned about her prospects. She looked a little down when she went to Mrs. Lloyd's to babysit. When Mrs. Lloyd asked what was wrong, Soria explained her dilemma.

"What would you like to do, Soria?" Mrs. Lloyd asked her.

"I'd love to travel, and I like working with people," Soria replied. "All I know is that I can't see myself cooped up in an office, typing and filing all day. I'm not the secretarial type."

"I can understand that, Soria; but you have real talents. When you start working full-time, I don't know what I'll do. It will be hard to find someone so reliable to take care of things. Not only do you babysit for me, but you're such pleasant company, too. You know, I'm on my way to the hairdresser. Let me mention your situation to Rose. She has all sorts of ideas."

Soria didn't think anything would come of their chat, but three weeks later she got a phone call from Mrs. Lloyd. "Soria, Rose has a great idea. A gentleman brought his young daughter in for a haircut. He's new in town and asked Rose if she knew of anyone who would like to do some light secretarial work. He's an internationally known architect and has settled here to establish what he hopes will be a comfortable, home-based business. You see, he's recently widowed and wants to work at home to be closer to his daughter."

Consider

What should Soria do? Outline the steps that you would advise her to take.

How to Prepare for Getting that Job

You have, by now, done a fair amount of preparation if you have been working on your career development. By the time you go job-seeking, you'll have pursued your interests and used your aptitudes to find an area of work that you enjoy, that you can succeed in, and that, in turn, will make you a happy person. What you need to do now is learn how to acquire the job that allows you to use that preparation.

The Résumé

What you need first is a method of relaying information about your education, experience, and skills to employers. The summary needs to be efficient, concise, and an attention-grabber. It needs to be convincing enough for the employer to want to meet you for an interview. The K.I.S.S. (Keep It Short and Simple) method is a good one to keep in mind when you are preparing the summary.

This summary is called a résumé. It should emphasize your strong points. Make it brief and easy to read, and organize it so that it highlights your most significant skills. We will discuss how to do this a little later.

The résumé must be neat, well organized, attractive, and up to date. You should include personal information about yourself, such as the address and telephone number(s) at which you can be reached. In addition, your employer will want to know about your

- career objectives

- education

- work experience

- related experiences

- interests and recreational activities

- memberships

- special achievements and awards

- references

To Do

Use the "Résumé Writing Guide" that follows and use it to organize your information. Before you begin to write your résumé, keep these points in mind:

- Keep it concise. More than two pages may "turn off" a potential employer.

- A résumé should be typed and neatly arranged on the page.

- Use standard-sized ($8\frac{1}{2}$" x 11" or 21.5 mm x 28 mm) paper. White paper is always acceptable; however, there has been a trend recently to use buff and lightly tinted paper to enhance the résumé.

Résumé Writing Guide

There are two parts to this guide. The first part will help you summarize your educational background, and the second focuses on your work experience. Provide the information requested for each of the parts. This will provide you with all the necessary data when you compose your résumé.

Educational Background

For each educational institution (high school, college, community college, university, training or vocational school) you have attended, provide the following information:

- Name and location of the institution.
- Dates of attendance.
- Diplomas or certificates received.
- Subjects studied.
- Grades awarded.
- Extracurricular activities.
- Awards or scholarships received.
- References.

Work Experience

Provide the following information for each of your work experiences. In addition to listing the jobs you have held, include any school-related or school-sponsored programs you have participated in (work-study, work experience, co-operative education, etc.). Also include any volunteer work or services you have performed.

- Name and address of the company.
- Dates of employment.
- Purpose or products of the company.
- Position you held at the company.
- Your duties and responsibilities.
- Skills you used on the job.
- Name and title of your supervisor.
- Starting and leaving salary.
- Reason for leaving.
- References.

Types of Résumés

There is no one "right method" of organizing the information in your résumé. Study some sample résumés. You will find that there tends to be some variety in the layout and organization of the material. You will probably find that there are two commonly used methods of ordering the information. Before you start your final draft, organize your information using one of these methods.

The first and most common method is the *chronological* method. Usually the information is in reverse chronological order, that is, beginning with the most recent event and continuing backward from there.

Another way of organizing your résumé is the *functional* method. Here you highlight your transferable skills, that is, those skills that are useful in a variety of jobs. This format clearly shows the potential employer what qualifications, skills, and experience you are ready to put to work.

Can you identify these two methods in the accompanying samples and see the differences between them?

Résumé Sample 1(a)
(Good chronological)

Adrian Scott Campbell
73 Grandravine Drive, Toronto, Ontario
M5K 1C8
Telephone: (416) 444-3815

EDUCATIONAL BACKGROUND

1988 YORK UNIVERSITY (TORONTO), FACULTY OF ARTS AND SCIENCE.
Graduated with a Bachelor of Arts degree in Business Administration.

1985 SENECA COLLEGE OF APPLIED ARTS & TECHNOLOGY (TORONTO).
Graduated with a Business Studies Diploma.

1983 MARIAN ACADEMY (TORONTO).
Graduated with a Secondary School Honours Graduation Diploma.

AWARDS

1986-1988	Dean's Award for Excellence in Business Management
1983	Ontario Scholar
1978-1983	Honour Roll, Marian Academy

WORK EXPERIENCE

1985-present (part-time)
HOLT RENFREW (BLOOR STREET STORE, TORONTO), SALES ASSOCIATE.
Duties: Working in the Gift Boutique Department. Responsible for display areas, record-keeping, and making cash/credit transactions. Learning the importance of setting priorities, especially during hectic sales periods.

1981-present (part-time)
YORK UNIVERSITY (TORONTO), LIBRARIAN ASSISTANT.
Duties: Assisting at the Reference Information Desk with inquiries about new and rare books.

1982-1985 (part-time)
HOLT RENFREW (YORKDALE SHOPPING CENTRE, TORONTO), CASHIER & SALES ASSOCIATE.
Duties: Worked in the Women's Apparel Department. Receiving, checking, and marking merchandise. Also responsible for cash register. Gained experience in public relations.

1980-1982
NORTHWESTERN GENERAL HOSPITAL (TORONTO), PHARMACY ASSISTANT.
Duties: Counted pills and delivered medication to patients in the hospital. Became aware of the importance of confidentiality in the workplace.

1978-1980
NORTHWESTERN GENERAL HOSPITAL (TORONTO), VOLUNTEER.
Duties: Assisted at the reception desk, greeting patients and visitors, answering inquiries. Developed good communication and interpersonal skills.

ACTIVITIES AND INTERESTS

1988-1989	Participated in York University's six-month Business Study Project in three European countries.
1987-1988	Vice-President of Business Students' Association, York University.
1984-1985	Member of Marketing Club, Seneca College.
1982	Student Council Secretary, Marian Academy.

I enjoy participating in water sports. Reading books, attending theatre shows, travelling, and singing are among my hobbies and interests.

Résumé Sample 1(b)

(Poor chronological)

Beverly M. Smithe
25 King Street, Vancouver, B.C.
V7V 5R2
Telephone: (604) 555-0123

EDUCATIONAL BACKGROUND

| 1989 | CARTER COLLEGE (VANCOUVER).
Finished Business Studies Part One. |
| 1988 | MEMORIAL HIGH SCHOOL (VANCOUVER).
Graduated with a High School Diploma. |

AWARDS AND SKILLS

1988	Heritage Valley Award for Excellence in Skiing Instruction
1984-1987	Honour Roll
1985	First place finish in the 1000m coxless fours at the Vancouver Harbour Regatta

Typing: 50 words per minute; driver's licence; computer programming; Standard First Aid (St. John

Ambulance); Heartsaver B (St. John Ambulance); Wilderness First Aid - Search and Rescue (Red Cross); Bronze Medallion (RLSSC). Languages: English and French.

WORK EXPERIENCE

December 1987-present **CENTRAL MEDICAL CLINIC (VANCOUVER), RECEPTIONIST.**
Duties: Answering the phone, booking appointments, filing records, and writing out bills. I learned the importance of being organized and knowing priorities.

January 1987-present **SHOPPERS DRUG MART (VANCOUVER), CASHIER.**
Duties: Worked as a cashier and helped in the pharmacy. I saw how a pharmacy works as well as performing cashier duties.

June 1986-September 1986 **SIMPSON'S DEPT. STORE (VANCOUVER), CASHIER AND SALES CLERK.**
Duties: Working as a sales clerk and cashier in the sports department. I became aware of the importance of being courteous to customers.

September 1985-June 1986 **B.B. FOODS (VANCOUVER), CASHIER AND GROCERY CLERK.**
Duties: Organized the fruits and vegetables into the correct sections and worked the cash register. I learned the importance of presenting products in the proper way and being on time for work.

ACTIVITIES AND INTERESTS

1988-1989   Member, Carter College Varsity Ski Team.

1988-1989   Member, Carter College Varsity Rowing Team.

1987-1988   Student Council Senior Social Rep, Memorial High School.

1982-1988   Member and instructor at the Vancouver Harbour Athletics Centre.

1980-1989	Member and instructor at the Heritage Valley Ski Resort. I enjoy playing sports. Skiing and sailboating and rowing, travelling the world, attending girl guide meetings, and reading are among my hobbies and interests.

REFERENCES
Available upon request.

Résumé Sample 2(a)

(Good functional)

Adrian Scott Campbell
73 Grandravine Drive
Toronto, Ontario
M5K 1C8
Telephone: (416) 444-3815

EXPERIENCE

June 1985-present(part-time)	SALES ASSOCIATE, Holt Renfrew, Bloor Street Store, Toronto, Ontario.
June 1981-present(part-time)	LIBRARIAN ASSISTANT, York University, Toronto, Ontario.
June 1982-June 1985 (part-time)	CASHIER & SALES ASSOCIATE, Holt Renfrew, Yorkdale Shopping Centre, Toronto, Ontario.
June 1980-May 1982 (part-time)	PHARMACY ASSISTANT, Northwestern General Hospital, Toronto, Ontario.
July 1978-May 1980	VOLUNTEER, Northwestern General Hospital, Toronto, Ontario.

SKILLS

LEADERSHIP

As a Sales Associate for Holt Renfrew, I was responsible for training new employees on cash/credit transactions and sales etiquette. In my second year of studies at York University, I was elected Vice-President of the Business Students' Association. In this position, I was jointly responsible with the President for co-ordinating policies and activities with other student organizations.

ORGANIZATION AND ADMINISTRATION

On the Business Studies Project, I was placed in charge of making the travel and accommodation arrangements for the whole group throughout the Project. It was also imperative that all members of the Project plan, develop, and implement the research required to obtain the material for the final report. I also have had the responsibility of organizing records of stock and transactions, both when I worked in the Pharmacy at Northwestern General Hospital and later at Holt Renfrew.

COMMUNICATION

The Business Studies Project required me to work together with other people to produce a single written report of our findings. As a Library Assistant, I was responsible for handling inquiries regarding the whereabouts of books. At Northwestern General Hospital I became familiar with how to deal with patients and visitors effectively. The knowledge I learned there in public relations was further developed in my work as a Sales Associate for Holt Renfrew.

EDUCATION

Bachelor of Arts in Business Administration, York University, 1988.

Business Studies Diploma, Seneca College of Applied Arts & Technology, 1985.

Secondary School Honours Graduation Diploma, Marian Academy, 1983.

References are available upon request.

Résumé Sample 2(b)
(Poor functional)

Beverly M. Smithe
25 King Street
Vancouver, B.C.
V7V 5R2
Telephone: (604) 555-0123

EXPERIENCE

December 1987-present	RECEPTIONIST, Central Medical Clinic, Vancouver, B.C.
January 1987-present	CASHIER, Shoppers Drug Mart, Gardenway Plaza, Vancouver, B.C.
June 1986-September 1986	CASHIER AND SALES CLERK, Simpson's Dept. Store, Vancouver, B.C.
September 1985-June 1986	CASHIER AND GROCERY CLERK, B.B. Foods, Gardenway Plaza, Vancouver, B.C.

SKILLS

LEADERSHIP
In the winter I teach skiing at the ski resort that I am a member of and in the summer I teach boating. In the past, I've assisted the local scouts and guides. People find it easy to get along with me; I'm not a very bossy person.

ORGANIZATION AND ADMINISTRATION
I had to type letters and billing forms. I also had to file away

patients' medical records. As a grocery clerk I had to organize the fruits and vegetables into the correct sections. When I teach skiing, I have to fill out the certificates for those people who passed the course. I also have to make sure that everyone has the proper equipment.

COMMUNICATION
As a secretary in the doctor's clinic, I must answer the telephone to book appointments for patients. It is my responsibility to type letters and other correspondence for the doctors. While working in the stores, I have to talk to the customers and answer their questions if I can. As a ski and boating instructor I have had to talk loud to be heard and understood.

EDUCATION
Business Studies - Part One, Carter College, 1989.
Graduation Diploma, Memorial High School, 1988.

References are available upon request.

To Do

1. Discuss both the chronological and functional methods in your class. Which method do you think an employer would favour? Decide for yourself which method you feel more comfortable using. Try that one first, but don't forget to try the other, too. The results may surprise you.

2. Before you complete your own résumé, examine the four samples that have been included. Which ones do you find more appealing? Why?

3. Make a list of résumé DOs and DON'Ts with a group in your class.

As you compose your résumé, keep in mind the following list of common faults that employers point out. These can spoil the impression you are trying to make.

- Too long
- Too brief or sketchy
- Errors in spelling, grammar, or typing
- Poorly organized
- Poorly expressed
- Overly confident
- Poorly photocopied or printed

The Letter of Application

When you send your résumé to a potential employer, it should be accompanied by a letter of application, or covering letter. This letter is a request for an interview. It should introduce you, express your interest in the company, highlight some of your special qualities, and indicate to an employer that it would be worthwhile to interview you. It is a brief introduction to your detailed résumé.

To Do

Study the "Guide for Writing a Letter of Application" and the two samples, which follow. The guide is written in the format of an application letter. Note that it contains three or four paragraphs and has a neat, uncluttered format. Each part of the guide explains what the letter of application should include.

Guide for Writing a Letter of Application

This guide resembles a letter of application in its appearance. Note, however, that the contents of each part explain what is to be included in that part of the letter.

Name and address of applicant
Date

Name and title of person to whom
letter is being written

Dear (Name of person, or job title if name unknown)

The opening paragraph must capture the reader's interest. It should also state the reason for the letter, specific interest, or job applied for, and where/why/how the applicant made the decision to contact this company.

    The middle paragraph(s) (there may be one or, at most, two) should explain in more detail the type of job sought and highlight the applicant's qualifications for the job. Remember that the specific details are in the résumé, which may be mentioned here as accompanying the letter.

    The last paragraph should make a request for an interview and may express the applicant's interest in and enthusiasm for working for this company.

Sincerely

Signature

and clearly typed name of applicant.

Enclosure notation (résumé)

Letter of Application: Sample 1

(Your address)
(Date)

Personnel Department
Dunkerly van Kolbe Designs Ltd.
29 - 2 Connell Court
Toronto, Ontario
M5C 3E7

Dear Sir or Madam:

This letter is to inquire about the Dunkerly van Kolbe Managerial Training Program.

I have heard that your company has an exceptional Managerial Training Program. I understand that a good marketing manager requires a thorough knowledge of the products or services a company offers as well as a familiarity with buyers' needs.

As the enclosed résumé indicates, I have been working in several job areas for the past three years on a part-time basis. During that time I have gained exposure to a number of situations that relate to marketing. I have been a ski instructor at Heritage Valley ski resort, which has given me an opportunity to practise public relations, too. I am familiar with the various kinds of advertising that are used today. I believe that these experiences, along with my educational background, make me a great candidate for your Managerial Training Program.

I look forward to the opportunity of talking with you to arrange an interview time for the Dunkerly van Kolbe Managerial Training Program.

Sincerely

Bev M. Smithe

Enclosure: résumé

Letter of Application: Sample 2

(Your address)
(Date)

Mrs. Shirley Anderson
Manager of Personnel Training
Dunkerly van Kolbe Designs Limited
29 - 2 Connell Court
Toronto, Ontario
M5C 3E7

Dear Mrs. Anderson:

This letter is being written to inquire about seeking a position in the Dunkerly van Kolbe Managerial Training Program.

I have recently returned from Europe, where I participated in a six-month Business Studies Project sponsored by York University. The project I worked on was a comparative study of the marketing strategies in the fashion industry of three European countries. While in France, England, and Italy, I had the opportunity to meet with the marketing and advertising managers of several of Europe's leading fashion designers. This experience has confirmed my desire to pursue a career in the marketing area of the fashion industry here in Canada. I have heard on many occasions and from several sources that your company has an exceptional Managerial Training Program. I understand that a good marketing manager requires a thorough knowledge of products and services as well as a familiarity with buyers' needs and that these aspects are included as part of your trainees' program of study.

As the enclosed résumé indicates, I have been working at Holt Renfrew Limited for the past six years on a part-time basis. My calibre of work there during this time allowed me to travel to Europe with the offer that I would be able to return to my position upon my return from overseas. My work in the retail area has allowed me to observe and analyse the effectiveness of various types of advertising. I believe that this experience, along with that

gained while working on the Business Studies Project,
makes me an excellent candidate for your Managerial
Training Program.

The prospect of becoming part of your company
excites and interests me very much. I look forward to
arranging a mutually convenient time to meet with you to
further discuss my suitability for a placement in the
Dunkerly van Kolbe Managerial Training Program.

Sincerely

Adrian Scott Campbell

Enclosure: résumé

In addition to using the guide, keep in mind these hints for
successful letter writing.

- Write your letter in rough, and go over it several times
  to check grammar, spelling, and composition before you
  type the final copy.

- Limit the length of your letter to one typed page.

- If your letter is slightly longer than one page, use only
  one side of the sheet.

- Plan the layout of your letter on the page so that it
  looks attractive and appealing to the reader.

- Apply for a specific job, not just anything.

- Make sure you spell correctly the name of the company
  and the name and title of the person to whom you are
  writing.

- Compose your opening statement so that the reader will
  want to read on.

- Use standard-size plain paper, not personal or fancy
  stationery.

To Do

1. Examine the sample letters of application. In class, discuss the strengths and weaknesses of each letter. Then, using the guide and the hints above, write your own letter of application.

2. After completing your letter, bring it to class and share it with your classmates so that you can evaluate one anothers' work and suggest improvements. Discuss any difficulties you experienced in writing your letter. Make the final adjustments to your letter of application, and then have your teacher evaluate it.

The Application Form

When you arrive at the workplace, you may be asked to complete an application form.

Consider

1. Have you completed an application form before?

2. Did you complete it in the office or did you bring it home with you?

3. Did you have difficulty completing any parts of it?

4. What did you do about the parts you had difficulty with?

To Do

Examine the two samples of completed application forms on pages 75–78. Using the "Guidelines for Completing Application Forms," which follow, evaluate each form. What errors do you find? Which completed form makes a more favourable impression on you at first glance? Which form makes a better impression after reading it? Why?

Guidelines for Completing Application Forms

- Read and follow the instructions on the form carefully.

- Print neatly, in ink.

- Complete all parts of the form; do not leave any blanks. (Write "N/A" where a blank is not applicable to you.)

- Give accurate answers.

- Give complete details of previous work experience.

- Come prepared: bring your résumé, covering letter, and any required documents with you so that you have all the necessary information, such as your social insurance number and reference names, addresses, and phone numbers, available.

- If you do not understand a question, ask what it means.

- Remember that your completed application form will create an impression about you; make sure the image it presents is the best. Complete your application with care, take your time, and re-read it for any omissions or errors before you pass it back to the employer. Take advantage of the opportunity to make a good impression.

To Do Obtain a standard job-application form from a company or your teacher. Fill it in, and then hand it to your teacher for an evaluation.

Completed Application Form: Sample 1

Poor—awkward phrasing; spelling errors; some sections not completely answered, others filled out when they should have been left blank.

APPLICATION FOR EMPLOYMENT					

POSITION APPLIED FOR: Any availabil

WAGES EXPECTED:

DATE AVAILABLE:

APPLICATION FOR EMPLOYMENT
PLEASE PRINT OR TYPE

SURNAME	FIRST	MIDDLE	PHONE	SOCIAL INSURANCE NO.
Smithe	Bev	M	5550,1,23	1,23,4,56,7,89

ADDRESS	STREET	TOWN	PROVINCE	POSTAL CODE
25 King street		mytown	B.C.	

EDUCATION RECORD:

SCHOOL	GRADE COMPLETED	DATE COMPLETED	COURSE STUDIED	DIPLOMA RECIEVED
HIGH: Memorial H.S.	12	Jan 89	General	Graduation
UNIVERSITY OR COLLEGE:				
TECHNICAL, VOCATIONAL, OR OTHER: carter college	3 semesters	Jan 89	Business	Business Part 1

EMPLOYMENT RECORD (MOST RECENT EMPLOYER FIRST)

COMPANY NAME / ADDRESS / REASON FOR LEAVING	EMPLOYED FROM / TO	SALARY FROM / TO	TYPE OF BUSINESS AND POSITION HELD	SUPERVISOR
Doctor's Clinic / Central medical centre / Still there	Dec 87 / —	$6.50	reception + billing evenings	Marion
Shopper's Drug mart / Garden way Plaza / Still there	Jan 87 / —	$5.25 / 6.25	drug store - helped in pharmacy too.	J.D. Bucks
Simpson's Dept Store / (Downtown Branch) / school starting	June 86 / Sept 86	$6.00 / 6.88	cashier and sales clerk	Bob Roberts
B.B. Foops / Garden way Plaza / summer job full time	April 85 / June 86	$3.80 / 5.65	cashier + grocery clerk	Ana Banana

HEALTH INFORMATION:

PRESENT HEALTH	ARE YOU WILLING TO UNDERGO A MEDICAL EXAM?	HAVE YOU EVER COLLECTED WORKERS' COMPENSATION DISABILITY BENEFITS? IF YES, FOR WHAT REASON
Good	YES ✓ NO ☐	YES ☐ NO ☐
WEIGHT 130 kg HEIGHT 5'6"		

REFERENCES:

LIST TWO PERSONS TO WHOM WE MAY REFER (NOT RELATIVES OR PREVIOUS EMPLOYERS)

NAME / OCCUPATION	ADDRESS	TELEPHONE	OFFICE USE ONLY
Harley Davids / Student	2002 Spaceway Drive Suite # 505	555 9876	
Susan Smithe / teacher	40 King Street	555 4321	

HAVE YOU EVER BEEN EMPLOYED BY THIS COMPANY BEFORE?		WHAT SOURCE REFERRED YOU TO THIS COMPANY?	DRIVER'S LICENSE?
YES ☐ NO ☑ IF YES ___ DATE LEFT ___ DEPT. ___		None	YES ☑ NO ☐ regular TYPE AND NUMBER
HAVE YOU EVER BEEN BONDED? YES ☑ NO ☐ IF YES June 86 DATE LEFT ___ BONDING COMPANY			
MAY WE CONTACT YOUR PRESENT EMPLOYER? YES ☑ NO ☐	ARE YOU WILLING TO RELOCATE? YES ☐ NO ☐ PREFERRED LOCATIONS		WILL YOU WORK SHIFT WORK? YES ☐ NO ☐
NAME OF FRIENDS OR RELATIVES IN OUR COMPANY			

CANADIAN MILITARY SERVICE:

BRANCH AND RANK	ENTRY DATE	DISCHARGE DATE	TYPE OF DISCHARGE	RESERVE STATUS

OUTSIDE HOBBIES AND INTERESTS, SERVICE CLUBS OR PROFESSIONAL ASSOCIATIONS: DO NOT LIST CLUBS OR ORGANIZATIONS OF A RELIGIOUS, RACIAL OR NATIONAL CHARACTER.

I really enjoy skiing and boating. I've assisted
in local scouts + guides, teaching these skills, reading

PLEASE ENTER OTHER DATA WHICH YOU FEEL MIGHT ADD TO YOUR QUALIFICATIONS FOR THE JOB SOUGHT, INCLUDING SPECIAL SKILLS, KNOWLEDGE OF BUSINESS MACHINES ETC.

I type well - 50 words per minute - very accurately
I like people and deal with them easily
I operate cash registers, word processors, telefax machines at my jobs. My employers have always liked me.

PLEASE READ CAREFULLY

I HEREBY CERTIFY, THAT, TO THE BEST OF MY KNOWLEDGE AND BELIEF, THE ANSWERS GIVEN BY ME TO THE FOREGOING QUESTIONS AND ALL STATEMENTS MADE BY ME IN THIS APPLICATION ARE CORRECT.

I UNDERSTAND THAT ANY FALSE INFORMATION OR CONSEQUENTIAL OMISSION CONTAINED IN THIS APPLICATION IS CAUSE FOR MY IMMEDIATE DISCHARGE. THIS INFORMATION MAY BE USED TO OBTAIN A FIDELITY BOND.

DATE march 89, Tues.   SIGNATURE OF APPLICANT BevSmithe

FOR OFFICE USE ONLY

MARITAL STATUS	DATE OF BIRTH	IN CASE OF EMERGENCY NOTIFY NAME	RELATIONSHIP
SINGLE ☑ WIDOWED ☐	31 01 60 DAY MONTH YEAR		
MARRIED ☐ SEPARATED ☐	NO OF DEPENDENT CHILDREN	ADDRESS	PHONE NO.
DIVORCED ☐		FAMILY DOCTOR	PHONE NO.

INTERVIEWERS COMMENTS

INTERVIEWER

DATE HIRED	DEPARTMENT	STARTING RATE	REG. HOURS	POSITION	DATE EMPLOYMENT COMMENCED

Completed Application Form: Sample 2

Good—neat, clear, complete, and *accurate*.

APPLICATION FOR EMPLOYMENT

POSITION APPLIED FOR	WAGES EXPECTED
management Trainee	negotiable
	DATE AVAILABLE April 1989

APPLICATION FOR EMPLOYMENT
PLEASE PRINT OR TYPE

SURNAME	FIRST	MIDDLE	PHONE	SOCIAL INSURANCE NO
Campbell	Adrian	Scott	4443815	654987321

ADDRESS STREET	TOWN	PROVINCE	POSTAL CODE
73 Grandravine Drive	Toronto	Ont	M5K 1C8

EDUCATION RECORD:

SCHOOL	GRADE COMPLETED	DATE COMPLETED	COURSE STUDIED	DIPLOMA RECIEVED
HIGH Marian Academy	13	May 83	Math & Business	Honours Grade 13
UNIVERSITY OR COLLEGE York University	3 year B.A	June 88	Economics Business	B.A Business Administration
TECHNICAL, VOCATIONAL, OR OTHER Seneca College	4 semesters	June 85	Business	Business Studies Diploma

EMPLOYMENT RECORD (MOST RECENT EMPLOYER FIRST)

COMPANY NAME / ADDRESS / REASON FOR LEAVING	EMPLOYED FROM / TO	SALARY FROM / TO	TYPE OF BUSINESS AND POSITION HELD / SUPERVISOR
Holt Renfrew / 50 Bloor Street West / still there - evenings & weekends	June 85 / present	$5.50 / $6.70	sales Associate Gift Boutique / Pat Peppertree 555-8132 - Ext 333
York University / 4700 keele Street Ross Bldg. / still there - Sunday only	June 81 / present	$2.80 / $6.15	Librarian Assistant new + rare books / Lidia wright - Smith 555 8080 - Ext 7132
Holt Renfrew / Yorkdale Shopping Plaza / offered transfer to downtown	June 82 / June 85	$3.75 / $5.00	Cashier & sales associate / Brenda Dupuis 741 0989 Ext 30
Northwestern General Hospital / 2018 keele Street / new job at Holt Renfrew	July 78 / June 82	$0.- volunteer / $3.00	help in reception — ended in pharmacy / Douglas Hooper 842-3120 - Ext 316

HEALTH INFORMATION:

PRESENT HEALTH Excellent WEIGHT 125 kg HEIGHT 5'7"	ARE YOU WILLING TO UNDERGO A MEDICAL EXAM? YES ☑ NO ☐	HAVE YOU EVER COLLECTED WORKERS' COMPENSATION DISABILITY BENEFITS? YES ☐ NO ☑ IF YES, FOR WHAT REASON N/A

REFERENCES:

LIST TWO PERSONS TO WHOM WE MAY REFER (NOT RELATIVES OR PREVIOUS EMPLOYERS)			OFFICE USE ONLY
NAME Dr. Al Fitcher — OCCUPATION family Doctor	ADDRESS Fitcher Medical Centre 500 Yonge Blvd . # 101	TELEPHONE 555- 0101 —	
NAME J.L. Pinelli OCCUPATION Teacher —	ADDRESS 55 keele Street #202 Marian Academy (H.S.)	TELEPHONE 341-2041 393-1111	

HAVE YOU EVER BEEN EMPLOYED BY THIS COMPANY BEFORE?			WHAT SOURCE REFERRED YOU TO THIS COMPANY?	DRIVER'S LICENSE?
YES ☐ NO ☑ IF YES N/A DATE LEFT DEPT.			Heard about excellent Management program	YES ☑ NO ☐ E I TYPE AND NUMBER
HAVE YOU EVER BEEN BONDED? YES ☑ NO ☐ IF YES Jan 81 DATE LEFT NWG Hospital Gift shop BONDING COMPANY				
MAY WE CONTACT YOUR PRESENT EMPLOYER? YES ☑ NO ☐	ARE YOU WILLING TO RELOCATE? YES ☑ NO ☐	Toronto - Metro Area PREFERRED LOCATIONS		WILL YOU WORK SHIFT WORK? YES ☑ NO ☐
NAME OF FRIENDS OR RELATIVES IN OUR COMPANY None				

CANADIAN MILITARY SERVICE:

BRANCH AND RANK N/A	ENTRY DATE N/A	DISCHARGE DATE N/A	TYPE OF DISCHARGE N/A	RESERVE STATUS N/A

OUTSIDE HOBBIES AND INTERESTS, SERVICE CLUBS OR PROFESSIONAL ASSOCIATIONS: DO NOT LIST CLUBS OR ORGANIZATIONS OF A RELIGIOUS, RACIAL OR NATIONAL CHARACTER.

Reading - Especially Design / Fashion / Self improvement books enjoy water sports / choir member - 8 yrs / Monthly Hospital volunteer

PLEASE ENTER OTHER DATA WHICH YOU FEEL MIGHT ADD TO YOUR QUALIFICATIONS FOR THE JOB SOUGHT, INCLUDING SPECIAL SKILLS, KNOWLEDGE OF BUSINESS MACHINES ETC.

- Responsible, Dependable employee / Steady, Enthusiastic
- Honour Roll student / Get along easily with people /
- Dean's award for excellence in Business Management studies / 1986 / 1987 / 1988 / Business Study project - 3 countries York University Europe - 6 months

PLEASE READ CAREFULLY

I HEREBY CERTIFY, THAT, TO THE BEST OF MY KNOWLEDGE AND BELIEF, THE ANSWERS GIVEN BY ME TO THE FOREGOING QUESTIONS AND ALL STATEMENTS MADE BY ME IN THIS APPLICATION ARE CORRECT.

I UNDERSTAND THAT ANY FALSE INFORMATION OR CONSEQUENTIAL OMISSION CONTAINED IN THIS APPLICATION IS CAUSE FOR MY IMMEDIATE DISCHARGE. THIS INFORMATION MAY BE USED TO OBTAIN A FIDELITY BOND.

DATE March 2nd 1989   SIGNATURE OF APPLICANT Adrian Scott Campbell

FOR OFFICE USE ONLY

MARITAL STATUS		DATE OF BIRTH	IN CASE OF EMERGENCY NOTIFY NAME	RELATIONSHIP
SINGLE ☐	WIDOWED ☐	DAY MONTH YEAR	ADDRESS	PHONE NO.
MARRIED ☐	SEPARATED ☐	NO OF DEPENDENT CHILDREN		
DIVORCED ☐			FAMILY DOCTOR	PHONE NO.

INTERVIEWERS COMMENTS

INTERVIEWER

DATE HIRED	DEPARTMENT	STARTING RATE	REG. HOURS	POSITION	DATE EMPLOYMENT COMMENCED

The Interview

Congratulations! You have been called for an interview. Your résumé has been a success, and the employer wants to investigate your suitability for a position. It will be very important to prepare adequately. The interview will be your opportunity to exercise your charm, present that positive image, and create a lasting good impression. If you are a little anxious, remember that it's normal to feel that way. The best way to be ready for your interview is to practise and prepare.

First, let's examine the purpose of the interview. The interview is really a two-way assessment. While you want to find out if this is indeed the job for you, the employer is looking for evidence to show whether you should be the future employee. To determine this, the employer will try to find out if your personality, experience, education, and training match the requirements of the job.

Consider some common criticisms employers have of students:

- Lack of preparation.

- Poor communication skills.

- Nervousness, overwhelming shyness, and a lack of self-confidence.

- Apparent lack of interest.

- An inability to "sell themselves" and to put their best foot forward.

Now review the qualities an employer looks for, in the exercise "Do You Have What It Takes?" on page 46. Remember, it is up to you to make all those character traits rate above average.

To Do

1. You have just been called about an appointment for a job interview related to the career you are considering. Describe how you will dress for this interview.

2. Make a list of what you will bring with you to the job interview.

3. The questions interviewers use tend to be quite standard; their wording may vary, but they are really looking for the same thing: "Are you the best candidate for the job?" Write out the responses you would give to each of the following questions.

   ● Why have you applied for this job?

- Why would you like to work for this company?

- What do you know about this company?

- What position are you most interested in?

- What qualifications do you have that make you feel you could be successful in this job and in this field of work?

- Why should I hire you?

- Are you willing to relocate?

- Are you willing to work up to the job you would like to do?

- What was your previous employment?

- Why did you leave your last job?

- What jobs have you enjoyed the most? Why?

- Do you prefer working with others or by yourself?

- Tell me about yourself.

- How do you spend your spare time?

- What are your future career plans?

- What are your salary expectations?

Answer these questions carefully, and phrase them as you would if you were speaking to the interviewer. Don't be vague in your answers, such as those about salary, interests, and qualifications. Good answers here will reflect your research and preparation. Prepare thoroughly. Your efforts will pay off!

4. Write down a few meaningful questions you would want to ask of the interviewer. Here are a few examples: When will you know whether you are hired? What benefits does the company offer? What is the potential for further education and/or training? Where does this job lead?

5. Once you have completed your answers to the interview questions, role-play a job interview with a classmate. You will want to do this twice, once as the applicant and once as the employer. When you are the interviewer, use the following "Interviewer's Evaluation Guide" to evaluate your applicant. Then discuss the results with him or her. Remember to be positive about the improvements that can be made. Do these interviews in front of the class, and ask classmates to offer suggestions for improvement. You will also learn a great deal from watching the other interviews.

   The following pages also include an "Applicant's Evaluation Checklist," which is for the applicant to complete after an interview. It would be helpful to look over both these forms before your interview.

6. Use the forms to make your evaluations. Discuss the results with your partner and your teacher, and then compare notes with the rest of the class.
   - What are the common weaknesses? Strengths? Concerns?
   - What are the solutions?

7. One very effective tool in interviewing is the video-tape machine. Try to videotape your interview. This will give you the opportunity to see yourself and give you a more objective view of how the mock interview went.

   Do make notes for yourself! They will be invaluable as you monitor your progress and develop a positive, competent image for future interviews.

Interviewer's Evaluation Guide

Use this guide to evaluate potential applicants. Review it before meeting the applicant. You should have received and reviewed the letter of application, the résumé, and the application form.

Keep this guide and the list of questions you plan to ask the applicant in front of you as you interview. Use a pencil during the interview to check off some immediate impressions or to make notes. Once the interview is over, review and complete the evaluation guide.

Explanation of ratings:
3: Excellent   2: Very Good   1: Acceptable   0: Unacceptable

Name of Applicant_____

Address_____

Telephone number_____

Date_____

Items	**Ratings**
Preparation	
Documentation:	
Application form _____	3 2 1 0
Résumé _____	3 2 1 0
Letter of application_____	3 2 1 0
Company research:	
Knowledge of company_____	3 2 1 0
Arrival	
Punctuality_____	3 2 1 0
First impression_____	3 2 1 0
Handshake_____	3 2 1 0
Appearance	
Appropriate attire_____	3 2 1 0
Facial expression_____	3 2 1 0
Posture_____	3 2 1 0
Manner	
Communication skills_____	3 2 1 0
Maturity_____	3 2 1 0
Personal Characteristics	
Alertness_____	3 2 1 0
Attitude_____	3 2 1 0

Enthusiasm_____	3 2 1 0
Genuineness_____	3 2 1 0
Manners_____	3 2 1 0
Sense of responsibility_____	3 2 1 0
Ability to "sell" oneself _____	3 2 1 0

During the Interview

Knowledge of the job_____	3 2 1 0
Interest in the job_____	3 2 1 0
Knowledge of the company_____	3 2 1 0
Clear speech and correct grammar____	3 2 1 0
Eye-contact comfort_____	3 2 1 0
Ability to answer questions_____	3 2 1 0
Ability to ask appropriate questions __	3 2 1 0

Concluding the Interview

Ability to conclude interview in friendly and polite manner_____	3 2 1 0
Applicant's interest at end of interview _____	3 2 1 0
Overall Impression_____	3 2 1 0

Notes_____

_____

_____

_____

_____

_____

_____

_____

_____

_____

_____

_____

_____

_____

Interviewer_____ Date_____

Applicant's Evaluation Checklist

After each interview, use this checklist to evaluate yourself. Try to be honest and objective so that you will be able to avoid repeating mistakes at your next interview.

For each item listed, indicate the description that best describes how you did.

Punctuality:	late/on time/early
Appearance:	well-groomed/satisfactory/ untidy
Posture:	good/fair/poor
Eye contact:	frequent/too frequent/ did not exist
Greeting:	friendly and natural/ average/anxious
Handshake:	firm and secure/wishy-washy/nonexistent
Poise and composure:	good/fair/poor
Attitude:	positive/average/negative
Personality:	pleasant and desirable in this line of work/satisfactory/ unsatisfactory
Self-assurance:	calm and confident/ average/self-conscious
Conversational ability:	fluent/average/awkward, difficulty expressing myself

Directness:	clear, unpretentious/ average/unclear
Comprehension:	good understanding of questions asked/average ability/slow to understand
Knowledge of the job:	excellent/average/poor
Knowledge of the company:	excellent/average/poor
Interest demonstrated:	sincere and direct/moderate/ none or little shown
Experience:	related experience/average/ not really related
Education:	excellent/sufficient/poor
Goals and aspirations:	clear and realistic/quite clear/questionable or unclear
Enthusiasm:	excellent and sincere/ some/none
Willingness:	excellent and open to new ideas/average/poor
Potential:	excellent — I think I will get the job/ very good — I have a good chance of getting the job/average — Maybe they will consider me /poor — I had better brush up and improve my...

- Did I thank the interviewer for his or her time?

- How might I have improved the interview?

● Did I send a follow-up letter to the interviewer?

To Do

Ask personnel managers to come to your class and speak about the kinds of things they look for during an interview. Have them conduct an actual interview with one of the students and then give feedback to the class. Ask them to explain the positive aspects of the interview and to suggest ways in which the student might improve. Have the interviewers use the assessment form included in the chapter; give them a copy before they come in. Or have them bring the form they use in their company. Then, while the interview is under way, have the students watch the interview. Later, students can compare their assessment of the interview with that of the personnel manager.

Preparation and practice are the best ways to ensure a successful interview. Here are some helpful hints to review before your interview.

The DOs

● Make sure your homework is done; review your information before the interview.

● Know your strengths and weaknesses.

● Dress in an appropriate manner.

● Be well-groomed.

● Act naturally.

● Be on time.

● Be honest, serious, courteous, and respectful.

● Look directly at the interviewer.

- Prepare relevant questions that you will ask the interviewer.

- Listen carefully and speak clearly.

- Appear genuinely interested.

- Use good posture when standing and sitting.

- Focus on the job and on your positive qualities.

- Bring a copy of your résumé.

- Bring a pen (or two) with you so that you can fill out any forms.

- Listen carefully to the interviewer so that you understand the questions.

- Remember to smile!

The DON'Ts

- Don't be late.

- Don't come unprepared.

- Don't chew gum or smoke during your interview.

- Don't fidget with your hands or an object.

- Don't lounge in your chair.

- Don't talk too much.

- Don't be too critical of yourself, apologize for your weaknesses, or blame others for them.

- Don't appear overanxious.

- Don't oversell yourself.

- Don't embellish your qualities or exaggerate the truth.

- Don't overemphasize salary and benefits.

- Don't become impatient.

- Don't lose confidence in the work and preparation you have done.

It seems like a lot to remember, but because of the preparation and the practice you have done, it won't be long before you hear those delightful words: "You're hired!"

Congratulations! But, as you probably know, your work has really just begun. Good luck on the job!

4

Entering the World of Work

After completing this chapter, you should be able to:

- Feel at ease and be productive during your first week on the job.

- Describe what it means to be a good employee.

- Describe an employer's expectations of a new employee.

Key Words

body language: the attitudes and feelings as conveyed by a person's movements and posture; also known as kinesics.

etiquette: forms of proper or polite behaviour; also known as "good manners."

feedback: the positive or negative reaction to a person's message, either verbal or non-verbal.

informal rules: unwritten rules that are followed as everyday rules for ordinary occasions.

orientation:	an introduction to familiarize people with new surroundings or circumstances.
Social Insurance Number (SIN):	the number assigned to every adult Canadian by the federal government to identify individuals for various purposes, such as income tax and social insurance benefits.
terminology:	the special terms used in an art, science, trade, or other specialized subject.

You've Arrived!

Well, here you are! You've finally made it successfully through the interview. Now you will need to make many other preparations to begin this new experience in the working world! As you start your new job, you will probably feel many things all at once — fear, excitement, apprehension, and eagerness. Your first day on the job is a little like a honeymoon. Everything is new and exciting, and you will be the centre of attention as you enter the workplace and take the first steps in getting to know your co-workers.

Much of what you do that first day will lay the foundation for the more complex tasks that will be assigned later on. Many people feel overwhelmed at this point. Others feel bored because they expect to start at the top with lots of responsibility. Any new job takes time to learn, and it may take some patience to take things one step at a time in your training.

Preparing for Your First Day on the Job

In order to make your day go as smoothly as possible, here are some things you can do:

- Make a list of what you need to do the night before you leave for work.

- Plan your time schedule — do you know how long it will take you to get to work? Be sure to allow extra time for unexpected events.

- On the evening before your first day on the job, decide what you will wear to work. Lay out your clothes so that all you have to do is put them on the next morning. This will keep you from panicking about how to dress for work. Dress conservatively if you are not sure what the dress code is. If you have a uniform to wear, check that it is clean and pressed; are your shoes clean?

- Organize the things you will need to take with you to work:

  —Do you need to make a lunch, or will you need lunch money?
  —Do you have enough money (or bus tickets) for trans-portation?
  —Have you listened to the weather report in order to know what to wear or take with you?
  —Are you clear on the directions to the workplace?
  —Do you have the telephone number of the workplace?
  —Do you know which department you are to report to (and which floor)?
  —Do you know who you are to report to when you get there? (Do you know how to pronounce the person's name?)
  —Do you have all the information that you have been asked to bring with you (for example, your Social Insurance Number)?

Becoming a Team Member

As a new employee, you are joining a team. A team is two or more people working together toward a common goal. Whether you work for a small or large company, it will be very important for you to become a good *team player*. The interests of the group will sometimes be placed ahead of the interests of the individual. The *common* goal you will all be working toward is winning — striving for the success of the business. A good working relationship develops when the goals of the individual and the goals of the business are compatible.

As a team member, you will be coached by your supervisor and co-workers. They will be working together to help you "fit in" as smoothly as possible. On your first day, you should be given some basic information about the job:

- the hours of work

- the lunch and break periods

- your assigned tasks, and how to complete them

- the locations of washrooms, the health room, the cafeteria, and other facilities

- the chain of command in your work area (the people you report to)

- your responsibilities

- your employer's expectations

- your pay dates, employee groups, special events, holidays, special procedures to follow in case of absence, and other useful information.

There may be other things that your employer will go over with you to help you to adjust to your new job. If you have questions that have not been answered, do not be afraid to ask. Some companies, especially larger ones, have standard orientation periods for new employees. For instance, large retail stores sometimes have a personnel instructor train new employees in special training rooms for a few days before the new employee goes on to the floor. This procedure not only reassures the new worker, it also benefits the company because the new employee is far more efficient and confident with proper training.

Getting Off to a Good Start

When you first start work, you will likely find yourself in the spotlight. People will usually be a bit more friendly; you'll get more attention, you'll get more smiles, and your co-workers will go out of their way to try to help you succeed. Your task is to try to keep the experience that way — to make each day *get better*!

Here are some tips to help you to accomplish that goal:

- When you arrive at work, greet your supervisor and co-workers enthusiastically. Smile, and be friendly and respectful.

- Listen carefully to instructions. Make notes if necessary, and then follow the instructions as they were given.

- Don't make assumptions. Be honest when you don't understand something. Don't pretend to understand something you don't understand. This only leads to frustration and possible mistakes.

- Follow your schedule at work. Take only the allotted time for breaks and lunches. Start and end your work at the scheduled times.

- As each task is completed, let your supervisor know. If he or she is busy, try to find something to do. Let your supervisor know that you are anxious to learn and ready to take on the next task.

- Keep a positive attitude. If things appear to be going wrong, don't panic. Ask for help. Any new task takes time and practice to master. Be patient with yourself and others.

- Start to get to know your boss and co-workers. Join in where appropriate in conversations, accept invitations to join your co-workers for lunch, and show an interest in them and their jobs.

- Take pride in your work. Give your best effort. Strive for accuracy and neatness even if you are given a tight deadline.

- Keep your eyes and ears open for the informal rules of the workplace. They can be very important in making you feel comfortable in your new job.

- Practise being a team player. Pitch in where necessary. Don't take the attitude, "It's not in my job description!" Instead, go the extra mile.

- Try to learn as much as you can about your job, the company, and the expectations of your employer each day. Don't worry if things seem to overwhelm you at the beginning. This is normal and will ease up as your knowledge of the workplace increases.

Case

Ryan arrived early for his first day at work. The interview had gone well, his orientation plan had been outlined at the interview by the personnel manager, and Ryan was eagerly looking forward to his first day on the job. When he got to the job site, he asked for Mr. Gone, his new supervisor, at the reception desk and told the receptionist that he was there to start in the Widget Department, just as he had been told to do. Everything was going as planned; that is, until the receptionist informed him that Mr. Gone had left yesterday for three weeks' holidays.

Ryan felt a little unsure of himself, but mustered his confidence as he was directed to the Widget Department. There he was met by Ms. Bizzi. She seemed a little upset at having to take responsibility for directing Ryan through his new job. "I'm very busy today!" she said, as she rushed him through endless rows of desks and everyone peered at him. "Mr. Gone has given me all this work to do plus his own, and I really don't have time to show you what to do. Here, sit at this desk and I'll be back in a half an hour."

Ryan sat at the desk for two hours before Ms. Bizzi returned. "Oh, dear! I'd forgotten all about you!" she exclaimed. "Why don't you just take the rest of the day off, and maybe I'll have time to show you some things tomorrow." With that, she left him sitting there, turned on her heels, and left.

Ryan felt utterly crushed and embarrassed. What had started out as a good day had turned into the worst day of his life.

Consider

1. What went wrong?

2. What should Ryan do now? What are his choices?

3. How could this situation have been avoided?

4. If Ryan were a co-op student, what should he do?

Case

Nancy arrived home after her first day at work, ready to quit. She told her parents, "This is not the kind of work I want to do. They are giving me chores that any kindergarten kid could do. If they think I'm going to do all their 'joe jobs,' they'd better think again. I know I can handle any job they ask me to do, if they would only give me a chance. I'm not sure I want to go back there and waste my time!"

Consider

1. Why does Nancy feels the way she does?

2. If you were Nancy's parents, what would you tell her?

3. What do you think the real problem is? Could it have been avoided? If so, how? If not, why not?

4. If Nancy were a co-op student, what should she do?

What Would You Do?

1. It is your first week on the job and you want to make a good impression on your supervisor. You want your co-workers to like you, too. What should you do?
   - Point out others' mistakes and correct their errors?
   - Show interest in your work?
   - Co-operate with co-workers?
   - Praise your co-workers to the boss?
   - Ask to be given only the tasks you are familiar with, so that you don't make mistakes?
   - Do something else?

2. Some co-workers make a suggestion to you about how you should do one of your tasks. Do you . . .
   - Do it the way they suggest?
   - Follow your own instincts and do it your way?
   - Tell them to mind their own business?
   - Tell them to do the job themselves?
   - Politely ask them to explain the suggestion?
   - Do something else?

3. During your first week on the job, a co-worker be-friends you and takes a special interest in making you feel comfortable. She fills you in on all the gossip at the workplace. Do you . . .
   - Thank her for telling you, and take notes?
   - Check out the facts with your co-workers?
   - Tell her politely that you would prefer to get to know others by yourself?
   - Do something else?

4. After a month on the job, you find that others do not give you the time and attention they did when you

first started your job. Sometimes you have nothing to do or are unsure of how to proceed. Do you . . .

- Look for another job?
- Ask for different work?
- Accept the fact that "the honeymoon is over" and do nothing?
- Ask for an appointment with your supervisor to discuss your concerns?
- Try to look busy and guess at what you're supposed to do, so that you don't disturb your supervisor or co-workers?
- Do something else?

Keeping Your Job

Entering smoothly into the working world can seem like a big challenge. Once you are there, an even bigger challenge waits — the challenge of holding on to your job. Many workers have lost their jobs because they didn't understand what was expected of them in the working world. Keeping a job can be hard work.

In order to survive on the job, you must learn skills that were not spelled out for you when you were hired. You must learn the rules of the workplace, or you will not survive on the job; you could either be fired or quit in disappointment. These rules fall into two categories: written and unwritten. The written rules of the workplace are straightforward and usually made plain to you. The unwritten rules are usually the ones stumbled upon, and if you break them they can cause endless embarrassment.

When you begin a new job, keep a journal in which to write down your observations about these unwritten but important rules and expectations in the workplace. As you learn them and put your new skills into practice, you will increase your chances of keeping the job you want, enjoying it, and moving on to new and better things.

Following are some of the rules and skills you will need to learn to increase your chances of success.

Respecting Privacy

In business, as in your personal life, there are times when other people's privacy should be respected. Sometimes there is a fine line between obtaining the information you need to do the job and participating in gossip. The following case illustrates the problem.

Case

Katarina began her first job working on an assembly line in a large manufacturing firm. The woman who worked beside her on the line, Sharon, was very friendly to her. She explained the "dos and don'ts" of the job and filled Katarina in on other co-workers on the line. Katarina enjoyed listening to her new friend because it helped to pass the time. Many of Sharon's stories about her co-workers were hilarious (perhaps even exaggerated), and Katarina got to know who she was working with more quickly.

However, Katarina soon noticed that others on the line began to avoid her. At first, she thought she was just being overly sensitive, but then she overheard some of her co-workers talking in the washroom. What they were saying did not make her very happy. They had noticed that Katarina was spending a lot of her time with Sharon, whom they referred to as the company gossip. Although Katarina did not gossip, her co-workers now thought that she was like Sharon and began to treat her differently.

Consider

1. Was any rule of privacy broken in this case? If so, how was it broken?

2. What aspects of respecting privacy concern you in your job? Share your concerns in class.

3. Make a list of dos and don'ts for a new employee starting to work in your company. The list should include two sections: the written rules of the workplace and the unwritten rules.

Communications

The importance of good communications on the job cannot be overemphasized. In order to do your work well and get along with your co-workers, it is important to know what good communications skills are and how to use them.

The basic communications skills are:

- reading

- writing

- listening

- speaking (verbal communication)

- non-verbal communication (body language)

Today, good telephone skills are a real asset in the workplace. They require a combination of some of the skills listed above, and we will deal with them in the conclusion of this section.

Reading

The ability to read effectively is a skill that develops with practice. Effective reading consists of reading quickly and accurately and understanding what you are reading. Reading skills are important not only in school, but also in the business world. People who achieve success in their work keep up to date on what is happening in their field. Much of this knowledge is gained through reading newspapers, books, trade magazines, reports, correspondence, and company materials.

Your job may require reading skills more than you realize. Are you required to read instructions from a manual to operate machinery or equipment? Do you have to read blueprints or maps? Do you have to read memos, letters, reports, notices, or purchase orders? Does your company have a bulletin board? It is important to read carefully in order to get the job done properly. Think back to the time when you filled out the application form for your job. Did it say, "Print in black ink"? How often have you caught yourself skipping over

important information such as this, only to find that you have to repeat the task because your mind was somewhere else when you read the instructions?

There are ways to improve your reading skills. Start with articles that interest you, and begin to read more often. When you read an article, practise skim reading. Skim reading is reading for the main ideas in an article or book. It replaces word-for-word reading and is useful for reading a large quantity of material quickly. It takes practice to learn but will be time well spent, especially when you are faced with a mountain of reading material.

Here are some points to keep in mind when practising skim reading:

- Choose an article you haven't read before. Start with an easy one on a topic that you are interested in, and work up to more difficult articles.

- Look over the article and read the main parts first. These are
    — titles and subheadings
    — first and last paragraphs
    — the main topic of each paragraph (usually the first sentence)
    — italicized or bold-face words.

- Avoid getting bogged down by details.

- Keep your eyes moving. Don't stop to re-read anything.

- Decide which parts of the article should be read thoroughly, either immediately or at a later date.

- After you have practised this technique for awhile, time yourself. Then see if you can judge how long it will take you to read a certain article.

- If you are reading an article that can be marked up, it sometimes helps to use a highlighter to mark the important points that catch your eye as you go along. This may slow down your reading, but it will help you retain points that you may want to review later on.

To Do

1. This week at work, observe the kinds of materials your co-workers read.

2. In your journal, list the varieties of material you have to read at your workplace.

3. Find and read an article about some aspect of your job. (You should be able to get it from your employer or from a local library.)

Writing

Not everyone wants or has to be a journalist in order to perform a job. Certain writing skills are important, however, in every job. Think of the number of times a day that you write something down — a telephone message, a letter, or a memo. Did you have to fill out a requisition, purchase order, or some other form? Did you have to take inventory and record the results? Did you fill out an order for a customer? Did you make notes at a meeting or write an article for a school assignment?

In business you will often hear the expression, "Get it in writing!" Writing things down provides documentation for present and future reference. Therefore, your writing should be accurate, clear, well organized, and concise. It should also be free of grammatical errors and spelling mistakes. Finally, handwriting should be legible and neat; no matter how brilliant it is, it will not be much good to those who cannot decipher it.

To Do

1. Pay special attention to your work journals. Are they well organized? Is your writing clear? Have you checked it for spelling or grammatical errors?

2. List the types of writing you are required to do at your workplace.

3. What types of written communication are used in your company? Ask a co-worker to help you find out if you do not know.

Reach
4. You have just informed your supervisor that you have been chosen to participate in a co-op student exchange program with students in Florida. You

want to bring a student to work with you for one week in March. You would like your supervisor's permission to do this. You would also like to return to Florida in April to complete the exchange for a period of one week with your exchange twin. Your employer has agreed to your request but asks you to put it in writing.

a. Write your employer a memo. Remember to use a courteous tone. Give this memo to your teacher for her or his comments.

b. Submit a one- or two-page essay to your teacher entitled "Why I Want to be a Co-op Exchange Student." This essay will be used by the selection committee to decide who will be able to participate in the co-op exchange program to Florida.

c. Write a letter to your co-op exchange twin in Florida. Tell her or him what clothes to bring to Canada, a bit about your job, what your school and community are like, and something about your home and family. Mention any special things that you plan to do together when she or he arrives. Submit this letter to your teacher for evaluation.

Listening

As a beginning worker, you will need to do a lot of listening on the job. Almost every day you will be given instructions about how to do your job. Being a good listener is one of the most important communications skills you can develop. The efficiency of many businesses might be doubled if only their employees knew how to listen well. Poor listening habits are the cause of many communication problems. They can also create problems for the company's image if you, as an employee, give the impression that you are not listening to a client.

Barriers to good listening occur when people:

● cannot hear what the speaker is saying.

- don't agree with what is being said. They begin to think about their own points of view and block out what the speaker is saying.

- interrupt the speaker with their own ideas.

- become distracted by the annoying mannerisms of the speaker.

- get tired of listening after a long period of time.

Can you think of other barriers to good listening?

To Do

1. Do you know what kind of a listener you are? Read this "Listener's Checklist" and identify both the good and the poor listening habits.
    - You start planning what you will say next while someone is speaking to you.
    - You don't really listen to what people are saying if you don't like them.
    - You pretend you are paying attention when you are really bored with what is being said.
    - You interrupt others while they are speaking.
    - You talk about yourself a lot.
    - You get distracted easily when people are speaking to you, especially if you're not really interested in what they're talking about.
    - You ask questions of the person speaking to you.
    - You have frequent "mental checkouts" when someone is talking, so that you find it difficult to remember what was said.
    - You try to see things from other people's point of view.
    - You maintain good eye contact when listening to someone.
    - You take notes when someone is speaking and miss some of what is said.
    - You give others a chance to speak.

2. List the listening habits you need to practise in order to improve your communication skills.

3. What are your listening strengths?

4. Explain why a good listener might make friends easily.

5. What is the difference between listening and hearing?

Reach

6. Ask some people who know you well to tell you what kind of a listener you are. (Don't interrupt them when they are speaking!) Afterwards, summarize what they told you.

7. Observe the listening habits of your co-workers. Who are the good listeners? Why? Who are the poor listeners? Why?

8. One way to improve listening skills is to paraphrase. Paraphrasing means repeating what someone said, but in your own words; it is not parroting. It helps both you and the speaker know whether you understood the message. Read the following statements, and then paraphrase them. The first two are done for you:

Speaker's Statement	Listener's Paraphrase
My boss doesn't respect me.	Are you saying that your boss doesn't appreciate you?
I'm afraid I'll fail this test!	You sound like you're anxious about being prepared for the test.
I think I speak too fast for these people.	
This place is a mess! I'm not cleaning it up!	
This is a real surprise!	

9. Paraphrasing takes practice. Find a partner, and have your partner say something to you. Paraphrase his or her statement, and have your partner tell you whether you understood the message. Reverse roles with your partner. Practise paraphrasing several statements.

Speaking

Has anyone ever said to you, "It's not *what* you said, it's *how* you said it"? If they have, your tone of voice must have revealed your feelings. Try saying the sentence below in several ways, putting emphasis on the emphasized word. How does the meaning change?

May I help you?

May **I** help you?

May I **help** you?

May I help **you**?

The way in which you use words can send a message that sometimes you don't really intend to convey. Have you ever found yourself arguing over a misunderstanding about what you really said? If you are aware of how you speak and how the words you use affect the message you are trying to convey, your communication will be more effective.

It is a good idea to "engage your mind before putting your mouth in gear." Being tactful when speaking to others is important in building good communications skills. Compare the following statements in the left-hand column with those in the right-hand column.

You're crazy!	I think I'm having trouble understanding what you mean.
You really know how to make me mad!	I really get upset when I hear you say that.
Your room's a mess! When are you going to clean it up?	I'm concerned about the untidiness of your room. Please clean it up.

Can you tell what is different about the statements in each column? The statements in the left-hand column put the blame on another person. They are "you"-centred. The statements in the right-hand column are "I"-centred and describe the speaker's feelings. They do not offend the other person by putting him or her on the defensive. When you try to say something, especially in a "touchy" situation, think carefully about what you would really like to say and try to use the "I" approach. After you have said how you feel, state how you would like things to be.

To Do

Read the situations described below and change the "you" statements to "I" statements:

1. It is your first day on the job, and your supervisor keeps looking over your shoulder while you are working. You wish that she would leave you alone. You feel you can handle the job on your own.

   "You" statement: "You're making me nervous."

   "I" Statement: "_____"

2. You have just started a new job and are told that everyone contributes to a lottery-ticket pool every week. You do not believe in buying lottery tickets.

   "You" statement: "You're not being fair."

   "I" statement: "_____"

3. You are new on the job and are performing the new tasks very carefully so that you do not make a mistake. You hear a co-worker telling the boss that you are slow.

    "You" statement: "If you'd never done this before, you'd be slow too!"

    "I" statement: "_____"

Learning how to speak properly can be a difficult thing, especially if you have poor speaking skills that have been overlooked by your family and friends, who accept you as you are. When you take your place on the job, people will not know you well, and you will have to use a more businesslike way of communicating. The demands of the workplace are that you speak to customers and co-workers courteously and grammatically.

Just as slang may be a language of its own at school, there is also a language of the workplace. It includes words and phrases that may be particular to a certain field. These words are sometimes referred to as "jargon," and they can be useful on the job. You must be careful, however, not to use too much jargon. You will want others to understand what you are saying, and jargon is useful only when your audience understands the words you use.

For effective speaking, keep these guidelines in mind:

● Speak clearly:
    — Avoid slurring your words.
    — Speak directly to your listener.
    — Project your voice so that you can be heard.
    — Don't mumble.
    — Don't speak too quickly.
    — Pronounce words correctly.
    — Avoid dropping word endings.
    — Don't stop partway through a sentence.
    — Use words that your listener will understand (avoid technical jargon when speaking to those who will not understand it).

- Use an appropriate tone of voice:
  — Be courteous.
  — Don't be sarcastic.
  — Keep a positive tone.
  — Modulate your voice to add variety and interest.
  — Avoid ending statements as if they were questions.
  — Be respectful.
  — Control the volume of your voice, especially when you're angry.
  — Try to hear yourself as others do.

- Use proper English:
  — Avoid slang.
  — Develop a large vocabulary.
  — Never use profanity.
  — Speak in a grammatically correct way.

- Have a plan:
  — Think through what you want to say before you speak.
  — Organize your thoughts.
  — Keep things simple.
  — Stay on the subject; don't wander.
  — Present what you have to say in an orderly fashion.

- Get feedback:
  — Ask questions to make sure that you're being understood.
  — Watch your listener for signals to guide you in sending out your message (for example, head nodding in agreement, eyes wandering because of loss of interest, confused expression.)

- Use appropriate body language to reinforce your message.

1. Practise making statements in two ways, to illustrate the right and wrong ways of speaking. Use the above guidelines as a reference.

Reach

2. Tape-record yourself when you speak. Play the tape back. Critique your voice and your presentation.

3. Have someone else critique a tape recording of a presentation you have made, and then critique a recording of a presentation they have made.

Non-Verbal Communication

Another term for non-verbal communication is "body language." It is often more powerful than speech, because some body language can be understood no matter what country you come from. Smiles and tears mean the same thing in any culture. Some body language, however, means different things in different countries. Gestures, eye contact, and body move-

ments can help or hinder a message, depending on how they are perceived by the listener.

It is, therefore, important to understand body language and how it affects your message, particularly because so much of it is unconscious and you may not be aware of it. Unlike verbal behaviour, non-verbal behaviour seldom lies. When you speak, people often pay more attention to your body language than to the words you utter. With this in mind, make sure that your body language agrees with what you are saying.

To Do

1. Following is a list of some body postures and movements. Discuss what these body movements mean to you. What could they mean to others? For each category, add any other body movements you can think of.

Standing
- hunched posture
- erect and relaxed stance
- with arms folded
- stiff posture
- other:

Sitting
- with ankles crossed
- with legs crossed at the knees
- slouching
- leaning slightly forward
- leaning far forward
- straight
- other:

Walking
- shuffling
- looking down
- with a bounce
- with head up
- rigidly
- with short strides

	with long strides
	awkwardly
	briskly
	other:
Handshake	limp
	crushing
	firm
	clammy
	other:
Mannerisms	biting nails
	twirling hair
	licking lips
	taking glasses off frequently
	fiddling with objects
	scratching
	chewing gum
	other:
Eye contact	direct
	staring
	wandering
	avoiding
	other:
Smile	natural
	smirk
	forced
	constant
	infrequent
	other:

Telephone Skills

There are some instances in which body language can neither interfere with nor enhance communication. In these situations, communication occurs through media such as the telephone. When you use the telephone, you rely totally on the voice. Facial expressions, gestures, and mannerisms do not show. Good telephone skills are an important asset in the business world.

To Do

Are you one of those people who think there is no need to learn how to use a telephone properly because you don't intend to become a switchboard operator? Do you think that it is just common sense to know how to handle a telephone properly? Take this quiz, adapted from one used by Bell Canada, to see how much you know about answering the business telephone properly.

1. What are the differences between face-to-face conversations and telephone conversations?

2. Why is it essential to answer business telephones promptly?

3. How soon after ringing should business telephones be answered?

4. Why do businesspeople always identify themselves (place of business, department, name) when answering business calls?

5. Is there a "best way" to hold the telephone?

6. What would you say to a caller if the person he or she requested could not come to the phone immediately? (Give the exact words.)

7. Why should the caller always be given a choice of waiting or being called back?

8. What are some reasons for not keeping callers waiting on the line? What should a caller be told while holding a line?

9. When the called person is not available, what information should the caller be given?

10. What can you do to assure the accuracy and completeness of a telephone message?

11. How can you avoid dialling an incorrect number?

12. What should you do if you reach a wrong number?

13. When making a call, how many times should you let the telephone ring before hanging up the receiver?

14. What should you keep in mind when hanging up the receiver?

Compare your answers with the following guidelines from "the experts" (Bell Canada) to see how well you are able to handle business telephone calls.

Pointers from the Experts

1. In *face-to-face* conversations,

- impressions of the person or company are gained through both sight and hearing.

- body language is apparent.

- the working environment is visible.

- the efficiency of the workplace can be observed.

- nervous gestures can cancel the effect of a good voice and pleasing personality.

- a crowded room can detract from the privacy of the conversation.

- people are less likely to take notes.

In *telephone* conversations,

- impressions of a person or company are based solely on hearing.

- body language is not apparent.

- the efficiency of the workplace can only be determined by the efficiency of the person handling the call.

- a good voice and pleasing personality can make a great impact.

- the communication seems more personal, regardless of the number of people in the workplace, because they cannot be seen.

- people are more likely to take notes.

2. It is essential to answer business telephones promptly because it lets callers know that the business values their time. It creates an impression of efficiency, is courteous, and lets callers know that someone is available and pleased to answer the call.

3. Many businesses insist that their telephones be answered on the first ring. Others say that they should be answered by the third ring because there is a six-second pause between rings on most phones. This sounds like a short time, and it is, but to the caller it seems much longer. Answering a call quickly gives the impression that the company is efficient and cares about the caller's time. It is good for the company's image.

4. Businesspeople do not simply say "hello" when they answer the telephone at the workplace. To let callers know they have reached the correct number, department, or desk, people who answer the phone should always identify the company by name if it is an external call, or give the name of the department or their own name if it is an internal call.

5. There *is* a "best way" of holding the telephone. The mouthpiece should be held directly in front of the lips, not under or on the chin. This makes it easier for the person on the other end of the line to hear you and gives a more natural-sounding voice. It also cuts out more room noise.

6. If the person being called cannot come to the phone immediately, the person answering the phone should ask if he or she can be of help and ask if the caller wishes to call back, leave a message, or hold the line until the call is taken.

7. Callers should always be given a choice to "hold" or call back because they may not be able to call back, may not wish to hold because they are busy, or may be calling long distance; or they may prefer to wait if making an urgent call.

8. It is important not to keep callers waiting on the line. Time seems to pass more slowly for the waiting caller, and waiting "ties up" the line and blocks other incoming calls. It also makes the caller feel that the company is not being sensitive to his or her time.

9. When the person being called cannot come to the telephone, the person answering the phone should offer to take a message and indicate when the caller can call back to reach the person who is not immediately available. It might be useful to give the caller the name of another employee who might be able to help.

10. To take a message properly, the person answering the telephone should write down all the information given or needed in order to return the call. This includes the name of the caller, the caller's business affiliation, the date and time of the call, the number at which the caller can be reached, any message left, any action taken, and the name of the person who took the message. In addition, any numbers or spellings of names should be repeated to check the accuracy of the message.

11. Incorrect numbers waste time — both the caller's and the receiver's. There are several ways to avoid dialling an incorrect number. Look up the number before dialling to check that it is correct. Dial only after you hear the dial tone. Dial carefully — do not use a pencil or pen; it can slip. If using a rotary dial, remove your finger from the dial so that the dial returns normally. Read the number carefully while dialling. Numbers can easily be transposed.

12. If you reach an incorrect number, don't just hang up. Tell the party you reached the number you dialled to

check whether the number is incorrect or you made a mistake in dialling. Apologize for your mistake, hang up, and try again.

13. When you hang up the receiver, allow the caller to hang up first. Hang up the phone gently — don't slam it down. Make sure that the receiver is properly in place, or you could tie up incoming calls.

14. Remember that the telephone rings once only every six seconds or so. When you make a call, allow it to ring at least ten times before hanging up. In doing so, you are still allowing people only one minute to answer the phone — not an easy task if they happen to be some distance from the phone. Be patient. Remember how you feel when you reach the phone after nearly breaking your neck, only to hear the "click" on the other end!

How did you do on the quiz? Whether you answer the phone at your workplace several times a day or only once in awhile, your employer will expect you to handle it in a businesslike manner. It doesn't matter what kind of company you work for or what your job is, good telephone etiquette is very important.

One of the most common complaints that employers have about their employees concerns personal phone calls. Succeeding in your job will depend on how quickly you learn the rules at work and use your common sense in applying them. Personal calls should be kept to a minimum and should only be made when absolutely necessary. Social calls should be discouraged. If your friends call you at work just to chat, let them know that you will call them later from home on your own time.

Case   Eunice seemed to be doing very well in her new position. She had been hired through a departmental transfer because she was known for her willingness to work hard and had expressed her eagerness to work in the sales department. Everything went smoothly until her third week on the job, when Eunice began to spend more and more time on personal calls.

The problem has become worse because Eunice does not answer all her own calls. When her line is busy, the call is "bounced" over to other staff in the same department. Lately, several people in the department have begun to complain that they answer too many personal calls for Eunice. In an attempt to cover up the number of personal calls she places, Eunice has begun to make calls from adjoining departments. Now other departments have told her that they do not like her making calls from their phones.

The number and length of her calls has increased so much this past week that Eunice is falling behind in her work. Today she has approached you, her supervisor, for permission to work overtime to catch up.

Consider

As Eunice's employer, what will you say? What will you do?

Success on the Job

What is success? It can mean many things to people; what does it mean to you? You have probably heard that there are a lot of things one must do to be successful. Movies like *The Secret of My Success* and *9 to 5* and TV shows such as "Designing Women" depict success in different ways. In the working world, however, success usually depends on a lot of hard work and the presence of some basic, but often overlooked, personal qualities. Following are some of the more obvious personal qualities that can contribute to success in the working world.

Making the Most of Your Appearance

You've probably heard that "It's not what you've got that's important. It's what you *do* with it that makes the difference!" Not everyone is a "10," yet it's not too difficult for most people to look their best. You don't need a lot of money; wearing clean, pressed clothes that are appropriate for your job will go a long way in making you feel good about yourself. Getting a haircut that suits your face will do wonders for it and hide the unflattering features that you think everybody sees a mile away. Wearing clothes that suit your build or your figure, instead of wearing something that just happens to be in style but doesn't suit you, will also help to improve your personal appearance.

Being well-groomed and paying careful attention to proper hygiene is very important. You may wear the best clothes in town, but if you have dirty fingernails or hair, your appearance will suffer. Using an effective deodorant or anti-perspirant may also be helpful. Make sure you know the difference between them when you purchase them, and try various kinds until you find one that works for you. If you have a problem with body odour and feel embarrassed about it because nothing seems to work, visit your doctor. Some people need special products or medical attention to help them solve this irritating and embarrassing problem.

It is important to choose clothing that "breathes." Any natural fabric, such as cotton, will allow perspiration to escape and your skin to breathe. Manufactured fibres do not breathe in the same way as natural fibres. Care should also be taken to clean your clothes regularly, so that any odour they absorb does not stay in the clothing. Regular bathing is a necessity.

Having Poise

Poise is the ability to be at ease in any situation. On the job, it means being at ease with your co-workers and customers. Having confidence in yourself is an asset. If you feel good about yourself, generally others will, too.

Being Punctual and Dependable

Attending work regularly and at the expected hours goes a long way when it comes to being successful on the job. The self-discipline it takes to be there when you are expected and needed tells others that they can trust you with other important responsibilities. It builds others' confidence in you.

Showing Initiative

Initiative is doing what you know should be done without having to be told to do it. Employers consider it a valuable trait in a worker; it means that they do not have to spend all their time looking over their shoulders to see whether you are working. They know they can trust you to go ahead with your assigned tasks on your own, and that you will let them know if you need assistance or more assignments. Having initiative also means that you are willing to work above and beyond the level normally expected on the job. You can show initiative by tactfully suggesting new and better ways of doing things or by improving yourself so that you can do a better job.

Case

Ian worked at a specialty paint shop, where vans and cars were brought in for custom paint jobs. He loved the job and put in long hours, often working past the time when he could have left for the day. He hoped that one day he would have his own business and wanted to learn all he could about the paint business quickly. So far, Ian had spent three weeks in the shop. His job was to bring the vehicles in, clean them up for sanding and priming, and assist with the taping.

This morning, things were going great. He could hardly wait until he got that first paint jar in his hands. He was ahead of schedule, and his boss had told him that he was doing a great job. Ian had almost finished cleaning up a car when his boss told him that he was going for coffee with a friend for half an hour. Ian waved and smiled and kept working. Within ten minutes he had finished the job, backed the car out of the shop, and looked around for the next job. He saw a van parked outside the garage doors, pulled it into the shop, and started to work on it.

Ian examined the van and wondered how some people had the money to spend on all these custom paint jobs. This van, for instance, sure didn't need a new paint job; the murals on the side panels were just like new! He managed to finish removing the mural from one panel when his boss returned. The boss poked his head in to see if Ian knew where his friend's van had gone. He had looked all over outside for it, but couldn't find it. He had parked it just outside the garage doors before they had gone off to have coffee together.

Consider

1. If you were Ian, how would you feel?

2. Was Ian showing initiative? Why or why not?

3. How could Ian have avoided such a situation?

Showing Enthusiasm and Interest

Employers like enthusiastic employees. Not only are they pleasant to be around, but they are usually the most productive workers. It would be great if we could be enthusiastic about our jobs all the time. But there are certain parts of every job that are boring or less than delightful for most of us. In spite of this, employers expect their employees to show an interest in all parts of their jobs.

If there are certain tasks that you really dislike doing, it will be easier if you get them over with first and then concentrate on the parts of your job that you do enjoy. It is unrealistic to expect that everything you are asked to do will bring you endless delight. The self-discipline you will learn in performing these tasks will help you to develop a more mature attitude on the job.

Being Courteous and Showing Respect

Showing respect for those you work with is a way of telling them that you care about how they feel. In business, deals are won through proper behaviour and the considerate treatment of others.

It is important to treat others the way in which we ourselves would like to be treated. Some companies even make it their business to give seminars on proper business etiquette, so that businesses can succeed both at home and in international markets. In some cultures, for example, it is considered rude to bring up the topic of business before spending a considerable amount of time in getting to know the client. This is not so in North America, where efficiency takes priority over good manners much of the time.

There are many issues involved in proper etiquette: knowing how to introduce people to one another, thanking someone, knowing how to address your co-workers (Mr., Mrs., Ms., or first name), and knowing how to behave in a variety of social situations, including those in which smoking is or is not a good idea. How much do you know about the etiquette of your workplace?

Being Honest

You probably assume that honesty is expected on the job. Some people, however, are dishonest with their employers. Honesty means using your work time properly, not taking company property, telling the truth, and using company resources in the proper way. Honesty is absolutely necessary for success on the job.

Being Loyal

Being loyal to your employer means that you do things for the good of the company. It means that what you say and do supports company goals. It does not mean that you think everything is perfect, but you will not publicly discuss things that should be kept confidential. You will keep things to yourself when it is in the best interests of all concerned and will "stick up" for someone or something you believe in.

If you cannot with all honesty say that you are able to do this in a particular job or workplace, it might be better to do a little "shopping around" until you find a company or employer that will command your respect and to whom you can offer your loyalty. You will be much happier working for an employer you respect.

Getting Along with Others

Getting along with others is of prime importance for success on the job. No one can do everything alone. The more complicated a job is, the more people it will take to keep things running smoothly. This means teamwork. Employers do not expect you to like everyone you work with, but they do expect you to do your utmost to get along with co-workers to complete the job. Petty conflicts have no place in the workplace. They undermine the efforts of everyone and create a miserable atmosphere.

The ability to take criticism without letting it interfere with a good working relationship is a sign of maturity. Listening to constructive criticism is important if you are ever to learn how a job can be done better. This involves listening carefully and politely to what is being said, thinking about how you can improve, and then acting on the advice. It means not losing your temper or your composure if you feel that you have been criticized unfairly. If you are confused by the criticism offered, ask your employer how you can improve. You will be treated more favourably if you approach your employer with an open mind and a willingness to learn.

Getting along with others also means being able to accept praise gracefully. You may feel embarrassed by the extra attention you receive when you are commended for your efforts in front of others, and you might behave awkwardly when praised. But remember that your good qualities are being appreciated and that those who are praising you are sincere. The next time someone says to you, "I like your outfit!"

don't say, "What? This old rag?" Instead, learn to say a simple "Thank you!" It's good manners, and it lets the person complimenting you know that you appreciate the sentiment.

Being Committed

Acquiring the self-discipline to follow through on a promise or on work or assignments isn't always easy, but it is necessary if you are to earn any credibility in your job. It has been said that "talk is cheap," and so it is. It really costs something to be good to your word all the time. Consistency, reliability, and commitment all result in earning the trust of your employer and your co-workers. It may cost you a little or a lot, but it will be worth your efforts many times over.

CHAPTER **5**

Adjusting to the World of Work

Your Personal Learning Objectives

After completing this chapter, you should be able to:

- Discuss ethical issues relating to the world of work.
- Understand how a paycheque is calculated.
- Identify safe practices on the job.

Key Words

budget:
a plan that shows the amount of money to be received and the purposes for which it will be used over a period of time.

ergonomics:
the study and design of work areas, tools, and furniture to enhance the health and safety of the worker.

ethics:
the branch of philosophy that deals with human conduct, the meaning of moral codes, and standards for judging right and wrong.

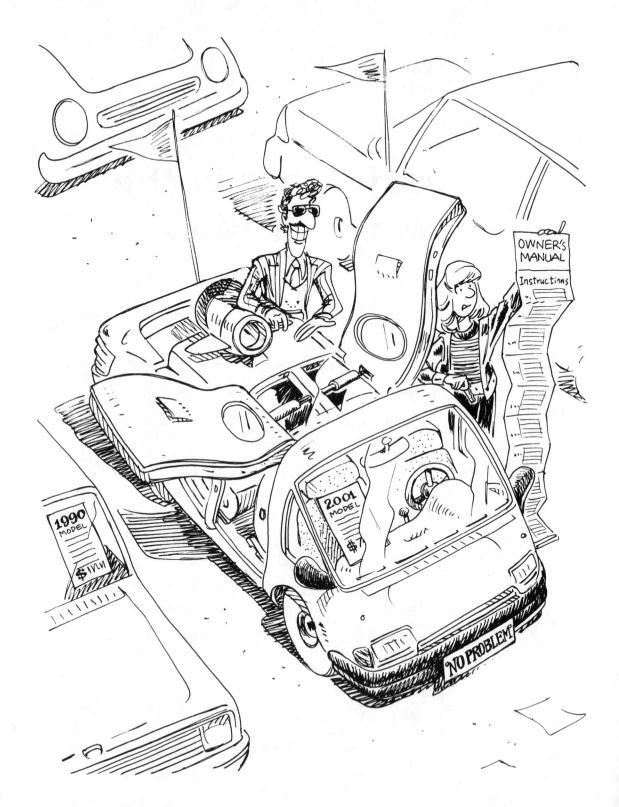

Ethics

Ethics involves an understanding of what is right and wrong and using that knowledge to make decisions in situations that may be questionable. A newspaper story that mentions a conflict of interest usually involves some question of ethics or good judgement on the part of the person involved. Exercising good judgement means looking at a situation from all points of view, thinking about how it might be construed by others, and then deciding whether it is in line with your values and what your company stands for. You will be happier at your job if what you want to do is in agreement with the company's values.

Case

Max's first week on the job had gone very smoothly. He was enjoying his job at the Beautiful Landscaping Company; his boss was very helpful, and Max really hit it off with his three co-workers. The job was varied. Some days he went into the office to do paperwork for ordering shrubs and landscaping supplies, and other days he worked outside at different locations. This job was for him! He liked working outdoors and being around others.

One day, as he was checking an order, he noticed a shortage of interlocking bricks in a customer's order. When he had recounted the bricks in the shipment, he asked one of his co-workers, Willie, what he should do about the shortage. Willie told him to forget it; it happened from time to time, so there was no need to worry about it. The office would straighten out the paperwork.

During the coffee break later that day, Max's three co-workers took him aside. "You seem like a cool guy, Max. How would you like to go into business with us on the side?" Max was pleased that they wanted him as part of their team. "What kind of business are you in?" he asked. "Well, let's just say that it's an extension of what we do here," Willie replied, and they all laughed. "What do you mean?" asked Max. "Remember that shortage you found this morning?" Willie reminded him. "Yes," said Max. "Well, the company is never going to miss a few bricks, is it? Once in a while we take a few and use them in our part-time business. You won't tell the boss, will you? After all, we *are* a team, and we have to work together on this."

Max didn't know what to say. All of a sudden things didn't seem quite right.

Consider

1. What would you do if you were Max?

2. Was Willie's concept of a team an accurate one? Why or why not?

3. If Max decides to report his co-workers, what might happen?

4. If Max keeps quiet about what his co-workers are doing but does not join them, what might happen?

What Would You Do?

1. Several of your co-workers have planned to go shopping at lunch time and they invite you to come along. They will be thirty minutes late in coming back from lunch. Do you . . .
   - Go with them?
   - Tell your supervisor what their plans are?
   - Say no and eat lunch alone?
   - Do something else?

2. After your first couple of weeks on the job, you notice that some of your co-workers become annoyed when your friends call you on the telephone during work hours. Do you . . .
   - Ignore them?
   - Ask your friends not to call you at work?
   - Tell your co-workers that it's none of their business who you talk to?
   - Ask your co-workers to tell your friends that you are not in the office?
   - Do something else?

3. It is your first week on the job at the Guzzler Gas Station. You have been told that your employer allows $2 spillage for every eight-hour shift. One night when you're working on the night shift, your co-worker brings his own car around to the pumps from the back of the station and puts in $5 worth of gas, the amount he figures wasn't spilled that day. He tells you he takes $5 worth of gas every night because the station only spills $1 every twenty-four hours and the owner has already allowed for $6 of waste over a twenty-four-hour period. Do you . . .
   - Tell your employer?
   - Keep your mouth shut?
   - Take your car in for a share, too, on the nights your co-worker isn't working?
   - Tell your co-worker that he should stop cheating the company?
   - Do something else?

Role-Playing Cases

Team up with others in the class to act out the situation described in each of the following cases. One person should take the part of the employer, and another the part of the student. Identify and discuss the important issues of each case after it has been played in front of the class.

Case

Employer: The new employee seems to be having his ups and downs. You notice that he enjoys working in the sports equipment area of the department and avoids assignments in toy and candy areas. Everyone must take turns in each area to provide good service to customers in all areas of the department. The new employee has just reported "bugs" in one of the candy compartments. The store opens in five minutes, so the candy compartment must be cleaned immediately. You ask the new employee to clean and disinfect the compartment quickly.

Employee: You work as a sales clerk in a large retail store. Your department includes toys, sports equipment, and candy and confectionery. You really enjoy the sports area. Today you have been assigned to work behind the candy counter. While preparing for opening, you notice "bugs" in one candy compartment. You report it to your supervisor, and she tells you to clean it out. You feel this is not part of your job. She seems to be picking on you because she has to throw out all the candy and resents the fact that you reported it.

Case

Employer: You have been extremely pleased with the progress of your new hotel clerk during her first month on the job. Her enthusiasm for her job and her career goal of managing her own hotel one day has impressed you. Because you wish to offer her more opportunities to learn the hotel business from the bottom up, you have arranged for her to begin training in other areas of the hotel. You know that this experience will help her meet her career goals. You want her to be successful, and you have been willing to "pull some strings" to arrange this extra training program for such a young, new employee.

Employee: You work as a hotel clerk in a large hotel. Your duties often change from one task to another. You enjoy sorting the mail, registering guests, confirming reservations, and taking messages. One day, you hope to manage a hotel. Your supervisor has complimented you on how well you have performed your duties at the front desk and has recommended further training in other areas of the hotel: catering, sales, and housekeeping. But making beds and waiting on tables isn't really your "thing." Why beat your brains out if you've made up your mind that the front desk is the only place you want to be? You want to quit rather than perform these awful duties.

Case

Think of a case relating to one of the topics introduced in this chapter or based on something that has happened to you on the job.

Your First Paycheque

Money is only one reason for working, but as you become more independent it will allow you to live in the style that you want. When you are hired for a job, you and your employer agree on a rate of pay. The rate may be calculated by the hour, the day, the week, the month, or as a yearly salary. It may be paid to you by cheque or be put directly into your bank account by your employer.

You may be waiting eagerly for that first paycheque to buy some of the things you've waited a long time for. However, when you get paid, you may discover that the amount may not be quite as much as you thought it would be. Read Jody's story to find out why.

Jody had big plans for Saturday. First, she would go shopping with her friends for clothes, then go off to the hairdresser, visit a specialty shop to buy a gift for her mom's birthday on Sunday, and finally spend her night out listening to her favourite band. She had already promised to pay her friend $25 for concert tickets. She had put a deposit on an outfit costing $140, and her hair appointment was going to cost her $20. How excited she was!

Jody knew that she had worked for thirty-five hours, and at a rate of $6 an hour she had earned $210. She calculated that she would have $25 left for her mom's gift — no problem. Friday came, and along with it her paycheque of only $168.55! When she saw the amount, Jody thought someone had made a mistake.

What Jody didn't know was that some money would be taken out of her pay each week for taxes, insurance, and other payments. These deductions from a worker's pay are made before the paycheque is made out to the employee. The total amount earned before deductions is called "gross" income. The amount left over after deductions, which is the amount the employee actually receives, is called "net" income. Some deductions are required by law, such as income tax and Canada Pension Plan contributions. Other deductions, not required by law, include health insurance payments, union dues, and charges for other special benefits.

Jody quickly went to her supervisor and asked her to explain why her cheque was for only $168.55. Her supervisor, Ms. Bucks, using a copy of the pay statement attached to Jody's cheque, explained why the deductions were made and where Jody's money went. Ms. Bucks showed Jody the company handbook, which explained the meaning of each part of her statement.

Jody wanted to learn more about the fringe benefits that were paid for by the deductions from her paycheque. She studied the company handbook carefully before her next paycheque arrived the following Friday. She also discussed her company's fringe benefits and paycheque deductions with her friends on Saturday. Jody thought carefully about her finances after that. She set some financial goals, planned a monthly budget, and opened her own bank account.

To Do

1. Obtain a copy of the statement of earnings and deductions that is attached to a paycheque.

2. Have the person you obtained the statement from explain the meaning of each of the items on the form. List each item and write out what each deduction is for.

Reach
3. Discuss your pay-statement notes in class. If possible (with permission), post your sample statement of earnings and those of your classmates on the bulletin board. Compare the examples, noting similarities and differences in various items and in the amounts deducted.

Case

Maybelle's friends have talked about taking a week-long trip to Acapulco during the March break in their senior year of school. Maybelle realizes that she can't pay for the trip out of her savings and goes to "good ol' Dad." Dad says, "Get a job, Maybelle. If you really want this trip, you'll have to pay for it yourself." After hours of pleading, Maybelle wins . . . well, almost. She agrees to get a job to pay for the trip, but because she needs the money soon, her dad has agreed to lend her $600, which she must repay before September.

To Do

Plan a budget for Maybelle. Calculate how much she must make (net) per hour or per week from April to the end of August in order to meet her commitment. Maybelle also has to repay her savings account for a $400 withdrawal she made in order to have spending money for the trip. How many hours a week would Maybelle have to work to repay her dad and her savings account? Remember that Maybelle must attend school until the end of June and can only work one evening a week and on weekends until July.

Playing It Safe on the Job

Young people going into the workforce now will probably spend at least thirty years of their lives on the job. It is also likely that they will change careers four to six times during their working years. Knowing how to stay healthy and safe from injury in a variety of work settings will reduce the risk of limiting a young worker's potential because of a serious accident or health problem.

The need for safety in some workplaces seems obvious to most people. If you are a butcher, you'd better know how to handle a knife or saw safely. If you work in a kitchen, you need to know how to handle utensils safely and be knowledgeable about putting out fires associated with cooking. If you are a custodian, you need to be aware of safety precautions for handling chemicals and make sure that no one will slip on litter or on wet floors. If you work in an office, you should know how to handle special equipment and be alert to other potential hazards.

Every job has special considerations. When you begin work for the first time in a new workplace, you should ask about safety precautions. Ask what the company's procedures are in case of fire. They may be very different from those followed in schools, but a company may also overlook relatively simple safety precautions; for example, fire drills are rarely conducted at the workplace. New employees should find out where the first-aid kit and the fire extinguishers are located, and should keep emergency phone numbers in an easy-to-spot place.

Every worker needs to know and follow the safety rules of the job. You should find out if any special equipment is required to protect you from being injured on the job. If your supervisor tells you to wear goggles while performing a task that may injure your eyes, make sure that you follow these

instructions. Some jobs require safety boots, hardhats, gloves, or other special clothing. When you are hired, your employer will usually tell you what clothing or equipment you need. In some cases, the company will supply you with what you need;

in other cases, you will have to purchase it yourself.

There are safe ways to perform all tasks. If you are a new employee, ask if there are particular procedures you should follow to perform an assigned task safely. For example, if your job involves lifting heavy objects, you should be given proper instructions about how to lift them. (There are legal restrictions on the weight of an object that a person can be asked to lift on the job.) Watch others, too, in order to learn how to do things safely. Usually, the longer you hold a job, the more familiar you become with proper safety procedures, and they are soon taken for granted.

Work injuries have many causes. Lack of proper safety instruction, faulty equipment, improper clothing, an inability to read, failure to follow prescribed safety procedures, and something as simple as being too tired to respond quickly to a hazard can all increase the risk of injury. Improperly designed equipment, furniture, and work areas can cause back injuries and other problems that may not be immediately recognized by the worker or employer.

What is being done to avoid needless injury to the worker? Some companies establish employee health and safety committees to protect the workers from unnecessary risks. Governments have passed laws concerning health and safety at the workplace, and employers must comply with these laws. Regulations exist that set out where, when, how, and to whom the laws apply. Some workers are covered by protective benefits if they are injured while working.

Special warning signs have been designed so that those who cannot read will understand them. At the workplace and in your community, look for these signs and symbols and make sure you know what they mean. For example, an octagonal figure (like a stop sign) means "danger," a square, diamond-shaped figure means "warning," and an inverted triangle means "caution."

The federal Department of Consumer and Corporate Affairs has the power to ban hazardous products and to regulate their sale and the way in which they are labelled. A system of symbols has been created to protect consumers from the harmful use of hazardous products. The four main hazards denoted on the labels of products such as bleaches, glues, sprays, cleansers, and polishes are: POISON, EXPLOSIVE, CORRO-

SIVE, and FLAMMABLE. The degree of potential harm is denoted by the shape of the figure that encloses the symbol.

To Do

1. Can you identify these symbols?

2. Create a safety poster that would be useful at your place of work.

If you feel that something in your job's tasks may injure you or someone else, report it to your supervisor immediately. Usually your supervisor will be glad you mentioned it. However, in many provinces, if the problem is ignored, you do have a legal right to refuse to do the unsafe work. This applies to all workers except police officers, fire fighters, and those employed in correctional or related institutions. In addition, people employed in hospitals, first-aid clinics, and public laboratories may not refuse unsafe work if in so doing they jeopardize the health or safety of another person. Workers can also refuse to engage in work activities that result in environmental pollution.

Refusal to Work

If workers believe that the work they have been asked to perform will endanger them or another person and they wish to refuse to do the work, there is a specific procedure that must be followed:

The Worker Immediately reports the situation to the supervisor and stays in a safe place.

The Supervisor Investigates the situation with the worker in the presence of another worker (a health and safety committee worker member or representative, or a person chosen by the union or by other workers).

If an agreement is made and the condition receives attention, the worker returns to work. If there is disagreement, the worker may continue to refuse to work if there are reasonable grounds to believe that anyone may be endangered if work resumes.

If the worker continues to refuse to work:

The Worker Notifies an inspector and remains in a safe place while the situation is being investigated. The worker may be assigned other work according to the terms of an existing collective agreement or be given other directions while the investigation is under way. The machine or workplace area is not to be used until the investigation is complete and a decision is reached.

The Inspector Inspects the situation in the presence of the worker, the employer, and a worker representative. He or she gives the decision in writing to the worker, the employer, and the worker representative as soon as possible.

In many areas, there are industry standards that have to be met. These standards exist to ensure a safe working environment. The laws and regulations governing worker health and safety are available from the federal Department of Labour, as are statistics on injuries. Current health and safety concerns include:

- toxic chemicals

- cathode-ray tubes (CRTs)

- air pollution

- ergonomics

- workers with special needs (such as wheelchair access)

- industrial standards

In a specialized, technical environment such as a shop, safety rules are usually stressed and are routine. However, general safety and housekeeping in seemingly safe environments such as offices are sometimes forgotten.

If your supervisors or co-workers tell you that there are no particular safe practices at your workplace, be wary. Often, health or safety hazards are not apparent. Some cannot be seen or felt, even though they cause harm; for example, carbon monoxide fumes and duplicating fluid can enter your body through your nose, mouth, or skin. Fatigue is a common hazard, and it can lead to accidents.

An office can be the scene of equipment-handling hazards, too, such as dangling bracelets inside a typewriter (there is sometimes a printed warning about this inside the machine); pulling out all the drawers of a filing cabinet at once (most modern filing cabinets are designed so that while one drawer is in use, no other drawers can be opened); and leaving electrical cords or personal belongings in places where someone could trip over them.

To Do

Look around your workplace and draw up a list of health or safety hazards. Then make a list of rules to avoid these hazards.

Case

Verie Careful is a co-op teacher who places students in many different workplaces. She believes that safety instruction is an important part of learning to succeed on the job. After her students' first week on the job, Ms. Careful has asked each of them to bring back to school a list of the safety rules they must follow at work. Their employers have adopted rules set out by the Industrial Accident Prevention Association. Here are some of the students' lists:

Jonas's list:

- Don't lift anything that is too heavy for you.
- When lifting, bend your knees, not your back.
- Always turn on the exhaust system when you are working at or near the barbeque pit.
- Wipe up all spills immediately.
- Always use the hand pads when working around hot surfaces.
- When removing lids from cooking pots, tip them so that the steam escapes away from your body.
- Use a paddle when putting pizza in the oven and removing it from the oven.
- Always make sure that the handles of cooking pots are turned inward from the edge of the stove.
- Make sure that frozen french fries are completely dry before putting them in the deep-fryer.
- Before going into the walk-in freezer, check that the inside latch release is working properly.
- Always wear your cap.
- If you are burned, immerse the injured part of your body in cold water immediately.
- Always use long-handled utensils when cooking meat on the grill.
- For any injury, always get first aid immediately.

- Always report any injury to your supervisor as soon as possible.
- Keep the floor free of obstructions.
- If you are working the last shift, always make sure that all stoves, barbecues, and fryers have been turned off, and check the walk-in freezer.

Todd's list:

- Be in good physical health at all times.
- Always take a warm, soapy shower and follow it with a cool rinse before entering the pool area.
- Never swim alone.
- Make sure that all diving is done in the deep end of the pool.
- Do not allow anyone to run or engage in horseplay around the pool.
- Clear the pool completely every thirty minutes.
- Check all pool equipment before giving it to swimmers.
- Know your limitations, and never try to exceed them.
- Keep emergency numbers by the telephone at all times.
- Report any damaged safety equipment to your supervisor immediately.
- Stay alert at all times.
- Finish each swim period with a shower.

Lisa's list:

- Never wear rings, watches, bracelets, or necklaces.
- Always wear a short-sleeved shirt or T-shirt.
- Always wear pants without cuffs.
- Always wear safety shoes.
- Always wear a cap to contain your hair completely.
- Wear appropriate gloves.
- Wear protective, safety-approved glasses.
- Wear the proper apron.
- Always take breaks and lunches when assigned.

- No overtime is allowed, except by special permission of the supervisor and with the approval of the health and safety committee.

To Do

1. For each of the above lists:
   - What do you think the co-op student's job is?
   - Give a reason for each of the rules.

2. Make a list of the safety rules for your job.

3. Discuss, with a co-worker or your supervisor, reasons for each of the job's rules.

4. Share your findings with the class.

Case

Ted works in a butcher shop and often lifts very heavy loads. He doesn't really mind that, since he considers himself strong and able to handle them. His boss is very careful that proper safety rules are followed. He has warned his employees that a serious injury could occur if the rules are ignored.

Last week a co-op student arrived for his work placement. Ted was placed in charge of the student and took a lot of time to instruct him about the safety rules. Today, when Ted was working in the back of the shop, one of the co-op student's friends came in to visit. Ted overheard the co-op student telling his friend that Ted was "always on his case" because Ted was so picky about how he handled the knives and saws and other equipment in the shop. The co-op student also told his friend how ridiculous it was that Ted insisted on washing the knives until there wasn't a drop of grease on the handles. He said he had no intention of being so fussy and had managed to slip some by Ted in the last few days.

1. If you were Ted, what would you do?

2. Was the co-op student right? Was Ted too picky? Why or why not?

3. Why do you think Ted wanted all the grease removed from the knife handles?

4. What could happen if the co-op student was injured on the job as a result of not following the safety rules?

Case

Natasia has just started to work at a restaurant. She is a very hard worker and willingly performs any tasks that she is asked to do. Her boss depends on her more than on the other workers. Natasia always arrives early and will work late to clean up, long after her co-workers have left for home. In fact, she does a lot more than her co-workers, and they have begun to get her to do all the jobs they dislike.

She often goes down into the basement to bring up heavy sugar bags. The stairs have no railings, and there are no backs on the steps. This week, she lost her balance and almost fell down the stairs. When she reached the top of the stairs and told her boss, he simply said, "Well, that was lucky for you, wasn't it?"

Natasia has also noticed that several other hazards exist in the restaurant. Often the floors are mopped when customers are entering the restaurant. This makes the floor slippery. Glassware is washed behind the counter by hand and is not properly cleaned when the workers are rushed. Cleaners and disinfectants are stored in the same cupboard as some of the cooking supplies. Natasia has seen the cook drop food on the floor, pick it up, and continue to use it without washing it. (Today it was a sliced tomato wiped "clean" on the cook's dirty apron!)

1. What can Natasia do to make the workplace safer?

2. If Natasia were a co-op student, what else could she do?

3. What do you think about the situation in which Natasia works?

4. If you were in Natasia's place, what would you do?

Reach

5. This will take some research. What law(s) or regulation(s) deal with this issue?

To Do

1. Test your "safety smarts" by deciding whether the following statements are true or false. State the reason(s) for each choice.

   - If you see a slippery spot on the floor, wipe it up yourself or report it to the appropriate person.
   - If there is a safety hazard with special equipment you are using, you should try to correct it yourself right away.
   - You should report co-workers who break safety rules.
   - You should always read instructions carefully before operating equipment.
   - If you hurt yourself on the job, you should report it to your supervisor only if you think it's serious enough.
   - When you're being hired for a job, it's okay to keep your health problems to yourself.

2. What should you do if . . .

   - Your employer asks you to lift a parcel that you believe is too heavy for you?
   - Your company is not observing industrial safety standards?

- A co-worker refuses to wear the prescribed safety equipment on the job?
- There are no fire extinguishers or first-aid kits at your workplace?
- A co-worker is injured on the job after ignoring company safety rules? (She asks you not to tell anyone.)

Reach

3. Talk to your supervisor about safety on the job. Report your findings to the class. Write and perform a skit to illustrate the importance of safety on the job.

4. List the telephone numbers in your area for: police, fire department, ambulance, family doctor, and other emergency services. (Keep a copy by the telephone both at home and at work.)

When an Accident Occurs

If you are involved in an accident at work, the first thing you should do is get first aid (if possible and practical). Then report your injury to your immediate supervisor and, if you are a co-op student, inform your co-op teacher at the school. Your co-op teacher or supervisor will then notify the local office of the provincial Workers' Compensation Board (WCB) or another insuring agent. A full report will be made to the WCB if the injury is serious enough to need medical attention.

Your employer must, by law, co-operate in reporting the accident and in arranging for transportation to your home, the doctor's office, or the hospital, if necessary. If you are disabled or require medical attention as a result of an accident on the job, your employer must notify the WCB within a certain length of time, which is determined by the province. It is important, therefore, for you to report any accident immediately.

Compensation for job injuries or illnesses as a result of work are determined by each province and are administered by the WCB. These regulations cover a wide range of jobs, but they exclude the following: casual workers and domestic servants, employees of financial and certain professional businesses, employees of charitable or non-profit religious organizations, workers in photographic studios, barber shops, and beauty parlours. Coverage for farmers varies among provinces; it can be either compulsory or optional. Usually there has to be a minimum number of employees in a group to qualify for coverage under the existing regulations, but just about any group can be covered by the compensation plan if the employer applies. Some workers are covered by private insurance plans for injury or extended illness. These plans usually require a minimum number of employees to join for special coverage, which is similar to the coverage offered by the WCB.

When a worker is injured and qualifies for benefits from the WCB, the level of compensation varies from province to province. If a worker is dissatisfied with the WCB benefits, he or she can appeal the decision to a review board within the WCB. There, the worker can complain in person or have a union official, lawyer, or other person present the case.

Other important services provided to workers through the WCB are a rehabilitation program to help injured workers return to work through special retraining, physical rehabilitation, vocational and social counselling, psychological testing, skills testing, selective job placement with a new or former employer, and arrangements for upgrading classes at an approved institution. Benefits such as these were first made available in 1949, when all provinces approved laws providing for Workers' Compensation. Under these laws, employers pay the premiums and employees receive the benefits by renouncing the right to sue their employers for damages if they are injured on the job.

To Do

1. Find out whether you are covered by Workers' Compensation benefits at your job. Who pays the premiums? What benefits do you receive if you are injured on the job?

2.   Find out whether there are other plans available at your place of work that compensate sick or injured workers. What are they? How do the workers join the plan? How much does the plan cost? What does the plan offer?

Reach

3.   Interview someone from the Workers' Compensation Board, the Industrial Accident Prevention Association, a health and safety committee, or another organization concerned with safety. What job-related injuries are the most common? What services does the organization offer to prevent worker injury?

UNIT Three

Living in the World of Work

CHAPTER 6

The Structure of Work

After completing this chapter, you should be able to:

● Describe what is meant by "company culture."

● Understand how a company is structured.

● Compare and contrast different organizational structures.

● Understand the role of unions and professional organizations in the workplace.

Key Words

culture: the way of life of a group of people at a particular time; includes their customs, beliefs, and arts.

image: an impression created by a person, group, or organization on the basis of its attitudes, policies, and practices.

liability: something that works to one's disadvantage; a handicap; a legal obligation.

structure: the way in which something is built, arranged, or organized.

Company Culture

When young people first begin a new job, they sometimes assume that all companies are the same and that a particular job will be the same regardless of the company they work for. Nothing could be further from the truth. A company is like a civilization; it has its own customs, rules, working conditions, and atmosphere. A company's culture consists of two basic components: its values (what it believes in) and its management style (the roles and behaviours it expects of its employees).

The Company's Image

A company may be very concerned with its image. That image can be influenced by many factors, some of which may not really reflect the true nature of the organization. Have you ever heard the saying, "You can't judge a book by its cover"? Many people forget this principle when it comes to choosing a place to work. They may not apply for a job with a company whose building is unattractive or whose furnishings are old because they want to work in an attractive environment. This may be a poor reason not to work for a company, because the company may offer other employee benefits that compensate for its unattractive surroundings.

A company's physical appearance is not the only thing that affects its image. Advertising also has a great influence on the way people perceive it. A company may wish to have a "fun" image, or it may want people to associate "professionalism" with its name. Some companies are very careful to hire only people who will reflect the company image, and they have rules to ensure that the image is upheld by their employees. For example, if a company wants to be known for its good service, it will try to hire people who are willing to "go the extra mile," who are courteous to customers, and who will do their jobs well. If a company wants a professional image, it may have rules about the clothing that employees are expected to wear on the job. This may be the reason for rules against blue jeans or for regulations demanding uniforms.

You should try to understand the image your company wants to project. Try to represent it accurately by following both the formal and informal rules of the workplace. The *formal* rules are those that are spelled out for you in black and white; they are usually clear and straightforward. The *informal* rules are those that you stumble upon as you progress in your job. They may be the more important ones in the long run because, even though they are unofficial, they will help you to feel that you "fit in." An example of an informal rule is given in the following case.

Case

Kirk had been with the company for six months. He was progressing well in his sales job and had been commended by his supervisor for his efforts and his high number of sales. One of the reasons that Kirk was so good at his job was that he listened carefully to what his customers told him and then acted on their suggestions to improve company service. His company had a Suggestion Plan that rewarded employees for ideas that improved company service and resulted in higher profits.

One day, after a customer had complained about a problem, Kirk decided to submit an idea to the Suggestion Plan that he thought would provide better service to the company's customers and save the company money. A month later, Kirk heard that he would be given a cash award of $1000 for his idea! He could hardly wait to share the news.

When he told one of his co-workers, the co-worker said, "Oh yeah, I heard. Good news . . . bad news. The good news is that one of us finally got a Suggestion Plan award. The bad news is that our boss is hopping mad. Didn't you know that he likes us to run our ideas past him before we submit them to the plan? He's afraid that someone will have a better idea than he does. He thinks it makes him look bad when he isn't the one to suggest new ideas or when he doesn't know about the ideas we want to submit. Now he'll be on your back for a long time!"

To Do

1. Can you identify the unwritten rule in this case?

2. What other unwritten rules have you stumbled upon or heard about at your job?

Working Conditions

Most people like to have pleasant working conditions. They appreciate facilities that make their jobs easier. Companies show a concern for proper working conditions by making available to employees the things that they feel are important. They may provide a company lounge for rest periods, a subsidized cafeteria, pleasant office colours, music, flex hours, short shifts, or such things as "quality circles" and job autonomy. The kind of working conditions that a company provides affects its image in the community and is a large part of what the company culture is all about.

Politics

The way in which an organization is structured and run determines the kind of political climate that exists in that organization. Just as the government of a country determines how decisions are reached and policies are formed, so the structure of an organization will affect its decision-making. It is important for you to understand the structure of the company you work for in order to understand your place or role in the company and progress within its political system.

The Company Structure

Before you accept a job with a company, try to discover what the company does, what its history is, what its products and services are, and how it is organized. This knowledge should help you make a wise decision about whether or not you would like to work for the company. Once you are "on the payroll," the more you know about your company, the more confidently you will be able to speak about company matters to your co-workers, your supervisor, and your company's clients. It will also help you progress within the company. If you intend to start your own business some day, the knowledge and experience you gain in your first jobs will be a great asset.

Companies are structured in various ways. The most common forms of company structure are:

- Sole proprietorships

- Partnerships

- Corporations (public and private)

- Co-operatives

The structure that a company chooses is influenced by factors such as size, economic considerations, and organizational goals. Each form of organization has certain advantages and disadvantages. Let's examine some of these forms of business structure.

Sole Proprietorships

A sole proprietorship is a business that is owned by one person. It is the simplest form of business organization. As a sole proprietor, you have these advantages:

- You can be your own boss. You have the flexibility to do what you want, when you want to do it. You can make your own decisions without having to get others to agree with you.

- You can determine your own income. Because you are the owner, you will be able to keep the profit made by your business. You will not have to divide it among other owners or investors. You can work as long and as hard as you want to make the business as profitable as you want it to be, and you can take as much risk as you want to take.

- Starting and closing the business is simple. In most places, all you need to start up a business is a licence. To close the business, the procedure is usually far less complicated for a sole proprietorship than for other forms of business organization.

Although sole proprietorship may sound good, there are some disadvantages you should consider before starting your own business this way or working for a business that is organized in this way:

- If it is a family-run proprietorship and you are not part of the family, you may find that your chances for promotion are limited. The owner may intend his or her children to inherit or manage the business, and there may be no room for you in their plans.

- Usually sole proprietors have fewer resources to draw on to manage the business. It may be difficult for them to leave the business for someone else to manage in their absence. They may have to rely on their own skills to make a success of the business and may find that this pressure is onerous. They may not be as free to come and go as they once thought they would be. If you work for this type of business, you may find that there is little opportunity to develop your management skills.

- There may be limited room for company expansion because of a lack of money. A sole proprietorship depends upon the owner's ability to raise funds, and there may not always be enough money available to expand. As a result, your ability as an employee to "grow with the company" may be limited to what the owner can afford at a particular time.

- Your success as an employee in a sole proprietorship may depend upon the owner's ability to absorb financial loss. A sole proprietor may lose all of his or her money if the business fails and be unable to continue the business if there is no one else to help. A sole proprietor can also lose all of his or her personal property if it has been used as collateral for business loans. This means that you should be concerned with the financial stability of a company, particularly if it is a sole proprietorship, when you consider where you want to build a career.

Partnerships

In a partnership, two or more people share the ownership of the business. Again, there are advantages and disadvantages in working for or becoming involved in this type of organization.

Some of the advantages of a partnership are:

- There is usually more opportunity for company expansion because of expanded resources — both financial and human. If the partners combine their strengths and efforts to reach a common goal, the business will be able to grow. As an employee of a partnership, your chances of growing with the company are better.

- It has often been said that "two heads are better than one." Different people bring different viewpoints to problem-solving, and this can benefit the organization and help it remain competitive. This can be a real asset to employees who are concerned with job stability.

- Each partner, by bringing different strengths to the business, compensates for the weaknesses of other partners. The skills of the individuals strengthen the effectiveness of the business in a broad way. As an employee, you may be able to relate to the different management styles of the partners even if there is one approach you don't like.

- If the business has financial difficulties, more people will share the losses and try to keep the business going. This can result in more job stability for an employee.

Although a partnership structure has distinct advantages, there are some disadvantages, too:

- Partners must share the profits. The percentage that each partner receives is usually determined when the business is formed.

- Partners may not get along well together, and arguments may arise over business matters, creating a tense atmosphere for employees. Sometimes this happens because partners are mismatched in abilities and one of them feels that the others are not doing their share of the work. At other times it happens because the responsibilities of each partner have not been clearly defined, and one partner feels that another is always interfering with his or her area of responsibility. Or the partners may have chosen to work with others who are too similar to themselves; and their weaknesses, when combined, do not match their strengths.

- When a partnership becomes unworkable, the business may have to be dissolved. If one partner decides to leave, the others may not have the money to buy out the departing partner's share of the business. The business might have to be sold and then started up all over again with new partners. This is very costly and time-consuming and can mean that jobs are lost. If the partnership is successfully dissolved without closing the business, the organization can still be hurt if the departing partner's skills or money are difficult to replace.

- Although profits are shared by the partners, so are losses. Although the partners' contract may set out the way in which profits are to be shared, the law states that each partner's liability for losses is not limited to his or her share in the company. One partner may have to cover the losses that occur as a result of the actions of another partner in the company. This can mean job instability for employees.

Corporations

A corporation is owned by stockholders who purchase shares, or stock, to finance the business. Under the law, a corporation has the same rights and liabilities as an individual person, but it is governed by a board of directors elected by the stockholders. The board of directors is responsible for choosing the corporate executive officers. These officers usually include a president, vice-president, secretary, and treasurer. They are responsible for carrying out the daily operation of company business and for putting into action the corporate policies established by the board of directors.

A private corporation is one in which the stockholders, directors, and managers of the corporation are all the same people. This is usually the case when members of a family form a corporation and control all the shares themselves.

A public corporation is one in which the shares of the corporation can be purchased by anyone who wishes to invest in the business. Most of these shares are bought and sold through the stock exchange.

A corporation, either private or public, has some advantages that may affect you as an employee or stockholder:

- *Greater growth potential.* Some of the largest companies in the world are owned by many investors, making it possible for the company to draw on greater financial resources than would otherwise be available. There is greater room for individual career growth in this type of company structure simply because of its size and diversity. As the corporation grows, the need for skilled personnel to operate the company efficiently increases. If you work for a corporation, your chances of "climbing up the ladder" into management or other areas of interest may be greater than in other business structures. You will also have the opportunity to observe a variety of management styles in action.

- *Greater job stability.* Because the corporation is owned by shareholders, if managing directors or executives leave, or if other owners sell their stock, the business can continue to exist without disruption. This is not the case in sole proprietorships or partnerships, in which the death or retirement of the owners could mean closing the business.

- *Limited liability.* Shareholders can lose only the amount of their investment and are not required to settle corporate debts if the business fails. This is not the case with partnerships or sole proprietorships, in which the debts of the owners could mean the closing of the business.

On the other side, corporations have disadvantages that should be considered.

- As an employee or small shareholder in a large corporation, you may feel that you don't have much input into the decisions of the company. The only way of increasing your control in the company is to purchase large numbers of shares — large enough to offset perhaps millions of other shares owned by shareholders with different ideas. This might require a huge financial investment. If you worked in a small corporation it might be easier to accomplish this, but it would still require large purchases of stock. You might find it easier to start your own company or retire with the funds that you would need to make such a large investment. The availability of stocks for purchase would also depend upon other stockholders' willingness to sell them to you.

- There are more regulations governing corporations than other forms of business structure. This is intended to protect stockholders and consumers. If you are employed in a corporation, this might mean that major policy decisions take longer than they do in partnerships or sole proprietorships. A corporation is less able to respond quickly to market demands, which puts it at a competitive disadvantage in remaining competitive in a changing marketplace.

Co-operatives

A co-operative organization, or co-op, is owned by members, who use the organization to market their products or buy products or services at reduced prices. The members of a co-operative are able to work together for a common goal that will benefit each member. Unlike the case in other profit-making organizations, membership is restricted to the users of the business and each member gets only one vote, regardless of the number of approved shares the member owns. If you work for a co-op or become a member of one, you will find that its growth is determined by the funds made available by the user-members. The more user-members, the larger the co-op, because there is usually a limit to the number of shares that each member is allowed to purchase. This can affect your opportunities for advancement within the organization.

To Do

1. What kind of company structure would you prefer to work in? Give reasons for your answer, referring to those characteristics of company structure and company culture that match your personal work style and career goal.

2. List the advantages and disadvantages of co-operatives that you should consider before deciding to work for one. (You may need to do some research to compile your list.) In class, discuss why you classified each point as an advantage or a disadvantage.

Reach

3. Consider a farm operation that is run as a family business. Report on the following: the structure that would be best for its organization, the pros and cons of your choice, and the skills required for a successful venture under your chosen structure. To do a proper job, you should talk to someone involved in farming to get his or her perspective. Include these insights in your report.

4. "Cottage industry" is a term often heard today. Define the term and give examples of the cottage industries you discover in your research. Prepare a report about one cottage industry by providing a complete profile of the business — its history, structure, culture, product, size, location, and other information. In the report's conclusion, summarize your impressions of the cottage industry you've chosen — would you like to work in a cottage industry? Why or why not?

5. If you wanted to start your own business — be an entrepreneur — what structure would you choose for your organization? Why? What would you want your company's image to be? What would your company's product be? What type of people would you hire? Why?

6. Research co-operatives more fully. Report on their diversity and give examples of their size, structure, services, and productivity. Include a comprehensive list of all the co-ops you discovered in your research, particularly local ones.

7. In class, create your own organization. Describe the structure you would choose and the legal process you would follow to establish your business in Canada.

Case

You have worked for the Better Company for ten years. You have decided to take a leave of absence from your job in order to return to school for a year.

To Do

1. In asking for this leave of absence, discuss the way in which your approach and the consequences of your action would differ if the Better Company were:

- a co-operative
- a corporation
- a partnership
- a sole proprietorship

2. Discuss the way in which your approach and the consequences of your action would differ in each of the above organizational structures if you were:

- an employee
- an owner
- a director
- the president

Organizing the Organization

Businesses can be small or large, limited or incorporated, national or multi-national. Whatever their structure, they all need some form of organization to identify the chain of command. "Chain of command" refers to the way work is organized and identifies those who have authority and responsibility within the organization.

Case Robin works as a co-op student in the accounting department of a large insurance company. She enjoys her work, and someday she wants to become a chartered accountant. There is only one problem: too many bosses. Whenever she is assigned work by her supervisor, other co-workers ask her to help out with their work. Often this is not a problem, and she willingly helps out in peak periods. However, it's now getting to be a daily thing for her co-workers to give her more and more of their work. Robin's last evaluation report showed that her production rate had fallen because she had not been able to complete her own work on time.

When Robin's co-op teacher came in to discuss her progress, Robin explained, "I don't want to hurt anyone's feelings by telling them that I won't help out when they need an extra pair of hands, and I don't want my supervisor to think I'm uncooperative, but I really don't know who I should take directions from. More and more, people just dump the work on my desk and expect me to have it done before I leave for the day. I've been staying late to finish my own work and theirs, too. I don't want to seem like a complainer. I really like it here, and I like the people I work with. What should I do?"

To Do

1. Discuss this situation with a classmate. What should Robin do?

2. Discuss this case with your supervisor. What should Robin's supervisor do?

3. If you were Robin, what would you want your teacher to do?

4. How could this situation have been avoided?

5. Draw up an organizational chart to show the chain of command at the company you work for or one you used to work for.

6. Would this problem be dealt with any differently if the company were:

    ● small?
    ● a sole proprietorship?
    ● a partnership?

Unions and Professional Groups

Unions

Why Have Unions?

Have you ever wished that you could switch your working days and your weekends so that you had to work only two days a week and got the other five days off? Most of us have! However, things were once much worse. In the nineteenth century, many people were forced to work long hours, seven days a week, under terrible conditions, for very little money. In Canada, workers started forming unions in the second half of the nineteenth century. They realized that there was a strength in their numbers that could bring about reforms for better wages, improved employee benefits, and better hours of work.

Before 1872, it was illegal to form a union in Canada. In that year the Trade Union Act of Canada was passed, making unions legal. Unions took on the task of bringing about political and social change as a responsibility to their members. Their efforts resulted in benefits such as workers' compensation (1915), a minimum wage (1920), old-age pensions (1927), unemployment insurance (1935), and medicare, health and safety protections, and laws to protect human rights.

Recently, some unions have been able to bring about changes in their collective agreements that add clauses on technological change, child care, equal pay for work of equal value, affirmative action, part-time work, and freedom from sexual harassment. Once collective agreements have been reached, their clauses are legally binding and enforceable by law.

Forming a Union

When workers want to form a union, they must follow a process set out by law. Labour-relations boards in each province administer a provincial Labour Relations Act. These Acts outline:

- The steps individuals must follow to join a union.

- What a union must do to represent those who wish to become members.

- What the employers must do to have a responsible relationship with a union.

Being a Union Member

People join unions for a variety of reasons. One reason may be to limit the power that employers (management) can exercise over them. Sometimes workers join unions because they belong to a trade or profession that demands union membership. Union members must pay union dues. Often these dues are taken out of the members' pay, just as other deductions are. Members are bound by the union's rules and regulations, but along with the worker's responsibility to conform to union rules comes the protection and rights offered by union membership.

Union members may also be subject to both provincial and federal legislation. For example, people working in fields such as banking, shipping, rail, interprovincial connecting work such as transportation and communications, and works considered "integral" to a federal undertaking are governed by section 91 of the Constitution Act. This means that bank workers, sailors, airplane and railway workers, and broadcasting and telecommunications workers are governed by the Canada Labour Code. This also applies to employees in the federal public service and federal crown corporations such as the post office. Workers in industries not specifically governed by the federal Parliament are governed by provincial labour legislation.

To Do

1. Could you, a student, form a local union? How?

2. Why would you, as a student, want to form a union?

Reach

3. Use a library or consult a local union steward or another resource to help you to write a job description of a union steward.

4. In your opinion, what type of person would make a good union steward? List some of the qualities that he or she should possess. Why are these qualities important?

Collective Agreements

A collective agreement is an agreement reached between a company and a union acting on behalf of the members of the union. Within a collective agreement, there are certain *mandatory provisions*, which may include provisions such as:

- a no-strike or lockout provision, which prohibits the union from "striking" and the employer from "locking out" employees during the term of the collective agreement;

- an arbitration clause, which provides a way of settling disputes about a violation or interpretation of the collective agreement that cannot be resolved by the union and the company on their own;

- a no-discrimination clause;

- a minimum length of time for a collective agreement to be in effect.

These mandatory provisions and all other provisions of a collective agreement must be negotiated and mutually agreed upon. The negotiations usually result in compromises, but once agreed to, the collective agreement becomes the law of the workplace.

Most collective agreements begin with a "preamble," a statement of the purpose of the agreement. This statement might say that the agreement is intended "to establish mutually agreeable wages and working conditions." Several goals may be included in the agreement. The agreement will also name the parties who will represent the union; this means that the company cannot bargain individually or directly with its employees. It must bargain through the union, which becomes the exclusive bargaining agent for those employees identified as the bargaining unit.

These provisions are usually found at the beginning of the collective agreement. Often included along with these provisions is a *management rights* provision. This clause acknowledges that it is a management function to control production, direct the workforce, and discipline or discharge employees when the employer has *just cause*. "Just cause" means a legitimate reason for disciplining an employee. The employer may be required to use "progressive discipline," in which the employee is given verbal or written warnings and a chance to correct the offending behaviour. However, progressive discipline may not be required in cases of particularly severe misbehaviour. Whatever the situation, management rights must be subject to, and consistent with, the collective agreement as a whole.

The labour movement believes that workers have a right to secure employment and a decent standard of living. As a result, unions have traditionally made "bread and butter" issues a bargaining priority. The employer already has an obligation under the provincial Employment Standards Act to pay a minimum wage, provide a certain amount of time for vacation, and grant time off on designated public holidays. These provisions are considered bare minimums that are inferior to the benefits gained by organized workers through collective bargaining. Unions have been able to negotiate such things as higher pay, better vacations, reduced hours of work,

company-paid medical and dental benefits, and employee pension plans to help workers share in the profits of their own labour and raise their families with dignity and financial security.

Other issues that may appear in a collective agreement are statements concerning:

- seniority (the length of uninterrupted employment with the company)

- job security

- new technology

- relocation allowance

- safety and health

- use of protective equipment

- affirmative action

- sexual harassment

- equal pay for work of equal value

- part-time work
- grievance procedures

Case

John has worked in a packaging plant for the past two months of his co-op placement. The workers are unionized. Lately, John has heard rumblings from his co-workers over a management decision to upgrade the plant. The company wants to replace its old equipment with modern, more efficient, computerized machines. It has offered to retrain its employees on the new equipment and has stressed that the new equipment will make their jobs easier. Many of the employees, however, do not want this new equipment.

John is confused about why the employees don't want to have brand-new machines, especially when it means that their jobs will be easier. When he asks his co-workers about this, he hears many concerns. Some employees are worried that they will not be able to learn the new technology and will lose their jobs. Some feel that once the new machines come, workers will be laid off because the machines will replace them. The company says that if the new equipment is not purchased, the plant will have to close down because it will not remain competitive in the industry.

Consider

1. If you were John, what would you say to your co-workers about their concerns?

2. If you were the president of the company, what decision would you make?

3. If you were the union representative, what would you do in this situation?

4. If you were John and the union workers decided to go on strike, what would your feelings be? What would you want to do?

Labour's Structure

The Canadian labour movement affects all industries and services, and unions are found in communities across Canada. That is because unions are "organizations of people." Labour's effectiveness rests in the hands of thousands of Canadians who voluntarily give their time to represent workers in all walks of life. Just as there is a chain of command within a company organization, so there is a structure for union organizations.

In general, the structure of organized labour follows that of governments in Canada. The central labour bodies act as the co-ordinating and lobbying agents for unions at the national, provincial, or municipal levels. Organized labour's goals are very often reached through central labour organizations that bring together a number of unions that have common interests and objectives. The power of these central labour bodies comes from their affiliated unions, which provide them with membership and money.

The Canadian Labour Congress

The national organization of unions is the Canadian Labour Congress (CLC). The CLC co-ordinates the activities of its affiliated unions at the national level. It oversees relations between the Canadian labour movement and the federal government in Ottawa and establishes relations with unionized workers world-wide.

The CLC consists of approximately one hundred national and international unions representing over two million workers. These national and international unions represent workers such as autoworkers, steelworkers, postal workers, and public employees.

The CLC frequently helps trade-union organizations in other parts of the world through the International Confederation of Free Trade Unions (ICFTU), an organization with about eighty-five million members. One of the ICFTU's most important functions is to establish and operate labour colleges that will help workers in Asia, Africa, and Latin America to form their own unions and engage in collective bargaining. Sometimes the CLC is asked to provide financial or other assistance to aid trade unions in other countries in their struggles with multinational corporations. As a result, the CLC's International Affairs Department has become increasingly important.

Provincial Federations of Labour

The CLC has an affiliated provincial federation in each province and territory. Each federation acts provincially in much the same way that the CLC acts nationally, pressuring and lobbying provincial governments and co-ordinating the activities of union locals. Because labour legislation is generally a provincial responsibility, each federation deals with matters affecting the labour legislation in its province. Provincial federations of labour are financed by per capita fees from their member locals. Local unions are entitled to send delegates to the federation's annual conventions, which reflect the concerns of the labour movement in each province. At these conventions, members determine federation policy in the province, elect officers, and decide which issues the federation will deal with that year.

The Labour Council

Just as the CLC relates to the federal level of government and the federations relate to the provincial level, so labour councils deal with matters of local government, municipal councils, boards, and commissions. The councils provide a way of bringing together local unions and enabling them to play a role in community affairs. They are responsible for carrying out the policies of the trade-union movement that originated in the provincial and national levels. The activities in which the labour council becomes involved include providing strike support for local unions, organizing union locals, fundraising for charities, and hosting CLC educational institutes.

Most labour councils in Canada have limited funds and no full-time staff. Their work is carried out by unpaid, elected officers and volunteers. As a result their effectiveness may vary from one place to another. Because the labour council is a "labour central" at the community level, councils are financed through per capita taxes on CLC affiliates in their community. Affiliation is not required, but all unions are encouraged to join.

The National or International Union (Affiliate)

The affiliate union is the labour organization that organizes and charters union locals, sets general guidelines for its locals, assists them in conducting their affairs, and co-ordinates their activities. For example, the affiliate might be the steelworkers' union, which will organize workers at a steel company, set up a local at the company, help them to bargain for a contract with the company, and help the union local conduct its day-to-day affairs.

The national or international union is financed by its local unions through membership dues. The dues pay for the administration of the union, strike pay, legal fees, staff salaries, and union activities.

Canada's international unions have their headquarters in the United States, partially because American union organizers followed American branch plants into Canada. Nevertheless, the leaderships of most international unions today recognize the political and legal differences between Canada and the United States and acknowledge that Canadian problems should be handled by Canadian officers. The Canadian sections of most internationals are now organized as separate Canadian districts. As a result, the policies of Canadian unions, whether national or international, are determined by local union conditions, requirements, and aspirations.

The Local Union (Lodge or Branch)

The local union is the base of the Canadian labour movement. Members of the local pay dues to and participate in its affairs, which include electing officers, bargaining and entering into collective agreements, keeping watch on contract administration, handling grievances, and implementing organizational programs at the local level. This is the level at which the union membership must participate in order to make the union effective.

Normally, local unions have a good deal of autonomy, because most collective bargaining takes place between the local and the employer of its members. There are certain exceptions to this practice; for example, bargaining may be conducted on a national or regional scale or, in some cases, by combinations of unions or locals and employer associations.

Locals vary in size, depending on the type of union to which they belong and the size of the establishments in which their members are employed. They usually meet either semi-monthly or monthly to conduct business and plan projects. Delegates to CLC and federation conventions and to regional and central bodies of their own unions are elected at membership meetings.

At every level, officers must be elected through a process regulated by the union constitution. Although these democratic procedures are not conducive to job security for union executives, they do keep the officers responsive to the needs and desires of union members. In other words, if the local union membership feels that the president or executive of the local is not doing a good job, the membership will have a chance to dismiss the executive and elect a new one during elections.

Dear Gabby:

I work as a co-op student in a graphics company, and someday I want to be a typesetter. My teacher had a hard time finding a placement for me because a lot of companies have what she called "closed shops." This one is an open shop. I don't really know what that means, but my supervisor said, "You don't want to know! I'm so tired of sitdown strikes, slowdown strikes, sympathy strikes, jurisdictional strikes, and wildcat strikes that I'll never work for another company if I have to join a union! Peace and quiet — that's all I want — and to get my job done without a hassle!"

I've seen some people on strike carry picket signs, but I really would like to know what my teacher and supervisor are talking about. I don't want to ask them in case they think I'm really out of it, and I don't want to get my supervisor all fired up again. Can you fill me in?

Baffled in Brandon

To Do

1. Write Gabby's response to "Baffled." Explain what each kind of strike is, and define "open" and "closed" shops. In your response, assure Baffled that she's not "out of it." Encourage her to find out more about how unions will affect her if she becomes a typesetter.

2. Give your letter to your teacher.

3. Discuss the points you made in your letter with other members of your class.

Reach

4. Interview a local union member from your community. Ask him or her the following questions:

   - How did the union get started at the workplace?
   - What are the terms of the collective agreement?
   - How large is the local union?
   - Who is on the local's executive?
   - What is the role of the steward?
   - Does the right to strike make unions too powerful?
   - How are grievances handled?
   - What are certification and decertification?
   - Which issues concern the local union?
   - When are meetings held, and what usually happens at them?
   - What does it mean to be a union member?
   - What has the local union done for him or her?
   - Does the member really feel he or she has a say in the union?
   - What is his or her feeling about open and closed shops?
   - What are the member's feelings about union membership?
   - Does he or she have any advice for students considering a job that has a union affiliation?

5. Research the Confederation of Canadian Unions (CCU). What is its purpose? Who belongs to it? Give a full report of your findings.

Professional Groups

Many career areas have professional groups that offer support to their members. These groups may or may not be associated with careers that have union affiliations. For example, there are professional associations for engineers, secretaries, and teachers. These organizations provide several valuable services to members, which may include holding meetings with other professional associations, providing printed materials for professional development, and setting standards for the profession. The structure of these organizations is determined by their constitution and the by-laws that govern their operation.

To Do

1. List all the professional organizations in your community. If you live in a large city, list ten.

2. Interview someone who belongs to a professional organization about their membership in the organization and the services offered to members. Present your findings to the class.

CHAPTER **7**

Learning the Ropes, Following the Rules

Your Personal Learning Objectives

After completing this chapter, you should be able to:

● Understand how Canadian law affects the worker.

● Understand the role of some government bodies in the world of work.

● Appreciate the relationship between ethical considerations and legal matters.

Key Words

conviction:	the state of being found or proved guilty of an offence.
discrimination:	an unfair difference in treatment.
fidelity bond:	an insurance policy covering losses caused by the acts of an employee.
right:	a just, legal, or moral claim.

Security in the Workplace

What Does Your Signature Mean?

Have you ever stopped to think how often you sign your name? Your wallet is almost certain to contain several examples of your signature. It appears on your driver's licence, your medical insurance card, your credit cards, your library card, and many other pieces of identification that you carry with you.

When you become an employee, your signature becomes more important. As you sign the job application form and other documents, correspondence, and forms for personal and business use, it is essential that you understand the power of your signature and use it carefully.

Some people are not careful with cheques. They may sign blank cheques in their cheque book, thinking that this will save time later on. This is a dangerous practice. If the cheque book falls into the wrong hands, anyone can fill out the cheques and cash them. Others do not fill in blank spaces with a line after signing the cheque. This is an invitation for a dishonest person to alter the cheque in some way. When you receive your paycheque, wait until you arrive at the bank with it or until you present it to some other person to be cashed before signing your name on the back of the cheque (this is called "endorsing" it). An endorsed cheque is as good as cash and, if lost, can be cashed by any holder ("bearer") of that cheque. It's a case of "finders keepers, losers weepers"!

Another good rule of thumb to follow in both personal and business matters is never to sign a blank form of any kind. Make sure you read every word of any document you are asked to sign, and before signing it ask questions about any terms you don't understand. Once the document is signed, you have committed yourself to abiding by its terms.

When filling out an application form, make sure you read the small print. Many application forms ask for your signature below a statement that declares that all information you have supplied is true to your knowledge. Supplying inaccurate information could result in the termination of your employment.

Once you are employed, you will be asked to sign forms relating to Workers' Compensation, income tax, Unemployment Insurance, medical releases, and other relevant documents. Your employer will probably explain the meaning of each of the documents you are asked to sign, but if not, you are responsible for asking questions about what you sign. On the job, you may have to sign invoices, letters, cheques, purchase orders, sales orders, or contracts. The rule is the same: know what you are signing!

Confidentiality

Confidentiality is important on the job. In some jobs it is so important that you may be asked to swear an oath of secrecy regarding all or certain aspects of your work. Treat it seriously. Your job may allow you to have access to confidential information that should not be discussed with anyone. The oath of secrecy may result in you being held accountable under the law if you divulge information about your job, and you may be dismissed from your job. Confidentiality on the job includes maintaining computer privacy. Under no circumstances should you tamper with computer access codes "just for fun." If you obtain classified or restricted information, whether it is in company files or on the computer, you could be in real trouble with the company and with the law.

Case   Sheldon worked as a co-op student in a data-processing firm. He considered himself a whiz on computers. One afternoon when no one was around, Sheldon decided to try breaking through the company's security code on his computer. He just wanted to see if he could do it. While trying to key in data, Sheldon's supervisor walked in and saw what Sheldon was doing. In a panic, Sheldon blurted out, "I was just trying to see if this computer works like mine at home."

Visibly upset, Sheldon's supervisor turned him over to company security personnel. After some questioning, Sheldon admitted that he fooled around with his computer at home quite a bit and was able to obtain bank information and school information, as well as a lot of other "heavy stuff."

To Do

1. What law did Sheldon break? (Hint: Ask a local police officer.)

2. What could happen to Sheldon if he is convicted?

3. Did Sheldon's supervisor treat him fairly? Why or why not?

4. What precautions could have been taken in school and on the job to make sure that Sheldon understood the consequences of his actions? Discuss this in class with your teacher.

5. What does "confidentiality" mean to you?

6. In class, discuss the meaning of confidentiality. What things are supposed to be treated as "confidential" on your job?

Case

Elizabeth worked as a clerk in a law firm through her co-op placement. In her job, she learned a lot about the affairs of people in her town. She knew how much her neighbour's house had sold for because her boss had been their lawyer. She knew that one of her friends at school had been in trouble with the law. Many other things that Elizabeth had access to in her job were considered confidential. Today, as she was doing her filing, her eye caught a document with her father's firm's name on it. Curious, Elizabeth read the document. She learned that her father's firm was in trouble. Upset, Elizabeth excused herself and went to the washroom to think things over.

Consider

1. Did Elizabeth break a rule of confidentiality by reading the document? Why or why not?

2. If you were Elizabeth, what would you do now?

3. Can Elizabeth tell her father about the document and its contents? Why or why not?

It is a good idea to discuss issues of confidentiality with your boss when you are unsure of what the rules are. You must be careful to honour your employer's code of confidentiality at all times. It is not appropriate to share confidential information with your teacher, your friends, your family, or others in the company who would not normally have access to that information. It is also not appropriate to discuss confidential information with co-workers who have access to the same information when that discussion is not part of the normal responsibility of your job.

Fidelity Bonding

Often employers will insure, or *bond*, employees who handle cash or other valuables as part of their job. A fidelity bond is a contract by which an insurance company guarantees to an employer that it will make up any financial loss caused to the employer by the dishonesty of an employee. Where bonding is not a requirement of the job, company officials trust their employees not to embezzle or misappropriate company property. Other employers who do not want to take the risk require their employees to be bonded, regardless of how honest they may appear to be.

In large corporations, fidelity bonding may be done on a "blanket" basis. This means that the employees are automatically covered by the bond when they take a job with the firm. Usually prospective employees are asked whether they are bondable and are required to complete a bond application as part of the hiring procedure. Once a person signs an application for bonding, the insurance company may investigate the applicant's background before guaranteeing his or her honesty to the employer.

Labour Laws

Although many workers are protected by the collective strength of unions, others who are not members of trade unions could be at the mercy of an unscrupulous employer. In order to make sure that workers everywhere get some protection, the federal and provincial governments have enacted laws concerning working conditions. These laws, called *labour laws* or *employment-standards laws*, are revised almost monthly to keep pace with the rapid developments in the world of work. As a result, some of the following examples may be out of date by the time you read them. Current revisions of the laws can be obtained from your provincial department of labour.

The Canada Department of Labour

The Canada Department of Labour was established in 1900 to prevent labour disputes, settle labour disputes, and to gather and publish information about labour. It eventually came to administer the Fair Wages Policy, which protected workers employed on federal projects, and other labour laws. In 1966, the Department of Manpower and Immigration became responsible for all employment-services policy except unemployment insurance. In 1976, the Canada Employment and Immigration Commission (CEIC) was established; it combined the programs of the Unemployment Insurance Commission and the former Department of Manpower and Immigration. The CEIC remains linked with the federal cabinet by a small department of employment and immigration.

Under sections 91 and 92 of the Canadian constitution, the authority to make labour legislation is shared by the federal Parliament and the provincial legislatures. The constitution outlines which industries and activities are to be regulated by the federal Parliament and which ones are under provincial jurisdiction. Federal legislation concerning labour is administered by the Department of Labour, the Public Service Commission, and the Treasury Board. The legislation can be divided into two main categories: (1) the Canada Labour Code, dealing with those who work for industries or other organizations under federal control; (2) the Public Service Employment and Public Service Staff Relations Acts, dealing with those who work directly for the federal government (federal public servants).

The Canada Labour Code

The Canada Labour Code was enacted in its present form in 1972. Parts III, IV, and V of the code apply to a wide range of employers, employees, trade unions, and employee associations that fall under federal jurisdiction in these areas:

- Interprovincial and international services such as:
  —railways
  —highway transport
  —telephone, telegraph, and cable systems
  —pipelines
  —canals
  —ferries, tunnels, and bridges
  —shipping and shipping services

- Radio and television broadcasting, including cablevision

- Air transport, aircraft operations, and aerodromes

- Banks

- Primary fishing, in which fishing is paid by wages

- Special undertakings that have been declared by Parliament to be "for the general advantage of Canada," which would include:
  —grain elevators
  —flour and feed mills, feed warehouses, and grain-seed cleaning plants west of Thunder Bay
  —certain mining and processing operations of strategic ores such as uranium

—certain individual undertakings, such as the Hudson Bay Mining and Smelting Company

- Most of the federally controlled crown corporations, such as the Canada Post Corporation.

The Canada Labour Code specifies fair employment practices, employment standards (concerning hours of work, minimum wages, annual vacations, general holidays, childcare leave, termination of employment, severance pay, payment of wages, garnishment of wages, sick-leave protection, bereavement leave, unjust dismissal, sexual harassment), safety regulations, and procedures for settling labour disputes. The code makes no distinction between full-time and part-time or casual employees. All are entitled to its provisions if they meet the qualifying requirements. The code establishes minimum standards with the intention that other rights or benefits will be negotiated between the employer and employee.

To Do

Obtain a copy of Part III of the Canada Labour Code (the part dealing with Labour Standards) from your local Labour Canada regional or district office.

1. Choose one section of Part III and read it thoroughly.

2. All the provinces set minimum employment standards. Find out what they are in your province in relation to the section you have chosen. Compare and contrast the provincial standards with the federal standards.

3. Report on the standards in your company in the area you have chosen.

4. In class, discuss your opinion of the Canada Labour Code Part III section you have chosen. How would you change it if you could? What parts of it would you keep? Why?

6.   Make a bulletin-board display about your chosen theme. Include both federal and provincial information.

The Canadian Charter of Rights and Freedoms

Before the enactment of the Canadian Charter of Rights and Freedoms, the first formal statement of civil rights in Canada appeared in the Canadian Bill of Rights, which was adopted by Parliament in 1960 under Prime Minister John Diefenbaker. The bill legally applied only to the federal government, even though it could override laws that conflicted with its terms. The government could also repeal or amend the bill as it saw fit.

Finally, in 1982, the Canadian Charter of Rights and Freedoms came into being. The Bill of Rights was not abolished by the Canadian Charter of Rights; they are both in force. The major difference between them is that the Canadian Charter of Rights and Freedoms takes precedence over all Canadian laws (it is "formally entrenched") and applies to both the provincial and the federal governments.

The Canadian Charter of Rights and Freedoms addresses the following rights:

- *Fundamental rights*, including protection of the freedom of conscience, religion, thought, belief, expression, assembly, and the press and other media.

- *Democratic rights*, including the right to vote and run for office and the right to hold regular elections.

- *Mobility rights*, including the right of Canadians to live and work in any part of the country they wish.

- *Legal rights*, including the right to life, liberty, and security of the individual according to the "principles of fundamental justice." This section guarantees the right of each person to be secure against unreasonable search and seizure, and says that a person cannot be detained or imprisoned arbitrarily. It also guarantees the right of any arrested person to be informed of the reason for the arrest, to retain counsel, and to challenge the detainment. The rules for fair trial are also contained in this section.

- *Equality rights*, prohibiting discrimination on the grounds of race, national or ethnic origin, colour, religion, sex, age, or mental or physical disability.

- *Language rights*, specifying that both English and French must be used in all federal institutions. It also guarantees minority-language education "where numbers warrant." In the provinces, the Charter recognizes the use of both official languages (English and French), and upholds bilingual provisions that are already in force.

The Canadian Charter of Rights and Freedoms is important because it will have a great effect on federal and provincial legislation in the years to come. Sooner or later, most people will have to consider the issues addressed in the Charter on a personal, public, or business level. Although both the federal and provincial levels of government retain the power to pass laws that may override some protections in the Charter, they must declare that the laws are being passed "notwithstanding" the provisions of the Charter, and these laws must be renewed every five years. This power does not apply to language rights, but only to laws concerning fundamental freedoms, legal rights, and equality rights. No province can "opt out" of the Charter. As situations arise concerning the issues dealt with in the Charter, the challenge to provide a clear interpretation of its provisions will fall to the courts. This may well be one of their greatest challenges in the future.

To Do

1. Obtain a copy of the Canadian Charter of Rights and Freedoms. (Hint: If you don't know where to begin, ask at the library.)

2. Read carefully one of the sections that particularly interests you.

3. In groups, discuss some of the issues raised in the Charter.

Reach

4. Discuss the Charter with your employer. What issues is he or she most concerned about?

5. Share your opinions and those of your employer with the class.

The Unemployment Insurance Commission

The first Unemployment Insurance Commission (UIC) cheques were issued to unemployed workers in 1942. Since then, further changes to the program in 1971 and 1976 have made it one of the most comprehensive in the world. You may notice when you look at the statement of earnings attached to your paycheque that a certain amount has been deducted for unemployment insurance premiums. The purpose of this deduction is to pay into a fund (subsidized by you, your employer, and the tax system) that will pay you an income if you become unemployed.

The amount deducted is determined by the amount of your insurable earnings (the total value of what you receive as payment for work that is classed as insurable employment). The amount you receive in benefits when unemployed is based on the income you received when you were working. The benefits are meant to be high enough to help you make ends meet, but low enough to encourage you to continue to look for work. As a result, you will be paid less than you were when you were employed.

To Do

1. Contact the local Unemployment Insurance Commission office and find out the following:

- Who is covered by UIC benefits?
- Who is not covered?
- What is the contribution system for UIC premiums?
- Who is qualified to collect benefits?
- How does one apply for benefits?
- How are UIC payments made to the unemployed?
- What rate is currently paid to the unemployed worker?
- How does the UIC catch "cheaters"?
- What is the sickness benefit?
- What is the maternity benefit?
- What is the retirement benefit?
- How does one appeal a UIC decision regarding benefits?

2. Discuss your findings in class. How do you feel about the UIC rules and benefits? If it were up to you, what changes would you make in the system? Why?

Case

Mona has worked as an employee of a janitorial services company for two years. She has just found out that she is pregnant, and the baby is due in seven months.

Consider

1. Is Mona eligible for UIC benefits?

2. For how long is she covered?

3. How would she apply?

4. Would she be eligible if she were self-employed?

Ethics in the Workplace

Wherever the law is spelled out for certain situations, people usually know what to do. However, there are situations in which things are not quite so clear. When employees are given certain privileges as part of a job or are placed in positions of trust, they often have to use their own judgement to decide on the appropriate action.

Case

Jake worked as a co-op student in a hardware store. His job involved a lot of heavy lifting, as well as some outside shop work. One winter day, on his way out to shovel the sidewalk in front of the store, Jake slipped on the ice and hurt his arm. The injury seemed minor, but just to be on the safe side, Jake visited a doctor to have his arm examined, as his employer had suggested. The doctor told him that everything was fine but to go home and rest for the morning and then return to work in the afternoon.

When Jake got home, he decided this would be a good time to take a few days off. He phoned his supervisor and co-op teacher and told them that he had to take the rest of the week off because of his injury. Then he flipped on the TV, made himself a hot chocolate, and stretched out on the sofa.

When Jake's parents arrived home from work that afternoon, they were upset that they had not been told of Jake's accident. They blamed the teacher for not calling them at work and were angry with the employer because Jake would lose a week of work. The next day they planned to see the principal to put plans in motion for Workers' Compensation benefits.

Jake was scared. Things hadn't turned out quite the way he had planned.

Consider

1. If Jake's parents go to the school principal, what process will be set in motion?

2. Who fulfilled their responsibilities in this case? Who didn't?

3. What outcomes are possible in this case?

4. What should Jake do now?

5. If Jake were to get away with this, what would the implications be? Consider everyone who might be affected, including Jake's fellow co-op students.

6. If Jake were to be "found out," what would the implications be? Again, consider everyone who might be affected.

Harassment

What Is Harassment?
The Canadian Human Rights Commission defines harass-

ment as a form of discrimination. It is against the law. Ten grounds of discrimination are prohibited by law:

1. sex
2. age
3. race
4. national or ethnic origin
5. colour
6. religion
7. disability
8. marital status
9. family status
10. conviction for which a pardon was granted

The Canadian Human Rights Act protects employees against harassment both at work and away from work, when incidents occur that are related to the job. It covers federal government departments, federal agencies, crown corporations, and businesses and industries under federal jurisdiction, such as banks, airlines, and railways. It is intended to allow people to work without being being hindered by discriminatory practices.

The Canadian Human Rights Commission has stated that harassment includes:

- verbal abuse or threats

- unwelcome remarks, jokes, innuendoes, or taunts about a person's body, attire, age, marital status, ethnic or national origin, or religion, etc.

- leering or other gestures

- condescension or paternalism that undermines self-respect

- unnecessary physical contact such as touching, patting, pinching, or punching

In order for a practice to be considered as harassment, the harassing practice must be reasonably perceived as a term or condition of employment. This includes practices that:

- interfere with a person getting a job, keeping a job, being promoted, or receiving training

- interfere with the provision of goods, services, facilities or accommodation customarily available to the public

- humiliate, insult, or intimidate any person

Harassment occurs when the person committing these actions against another person should know that they would be unwelcome.

Sexual Harassment

The Canada Labour Code defines sexual harassment as: "any conduct, comment, gesture or contact of a sexual nature that is likely to cause offence or humiliation to any employee; or that might, on reasonable grounds, be perceived by that employee as placing a condition of a sexual nature on employment or on any opportunity for training or promotion."

Under the code every employee in Canada is entitled to work free of harassment.

The Employer's Responsibilities

Canada's labour standards require that employers make every reasonable effort to ensure that no employee is subjected to sexual harassment. In fact, employers must establish a policy on harassment and make every person under their direction aware of this policy. The policy must include all of these items:

- a definition of sexual harassment that reflects the meaning stated in the code

- a statement that every employee is entitled to work free of harassment

- a statement that the employer will make every effort to ensure that no employee is subjected to sexual harassment

- a statement that the employer will take disciplinary action against any person under its direction who subjects any employee to sexual harassment

- a statement to explain how complaints of sexual harassment may be brought to the attention of the employer

- a statement guaranteeing the confidentiality of the complainant's identity

- an explanation of employees' rights under the Canadian Human Rights Act.

Harassment can be a complicated and controversial subject in the work environment. It is important to know what your rights are and to learn about your responsibilities. You must become a knowledgeable worker if you are to exercise your freedoms wisely.

To Do

1. Describe a situation you know of that involved harassment. What provision of the Canadian Human Rights Act regarding harassment was violated?

2. If you were a victim of harassment, what steps would you take to deal with the situation?

Reach

3. Here's your chance to write a "Case" about a situation in which harassment occurs. Call it "The Bully." Present your case to the class for discussion.

4. Write a paper about harassment in the workplace, focusing on one of the following issues: daycare, multiculturalism, disabled workers, single parents, senior citizens, or minority groups. Reflect on events that you have observed or thought about, and include facts relating to the issue you have chosen as well as your opinion about the issue.

CHAPTER 8

Surviving in the World of Work

After completing this chapter, you should be able to:

- Understand the importance of developing your skills on the job.

- Know how to prepare yourself for evaluation.

- Set goals.

- Understand what your needs are and how they relate to job satisfaction.

- Measure your growth progress.

Key Words

hierarchy: the organization of people or things by rank.

motivation: the state of being moved to action.

Develop Your Skills

In school, your teacher probably reminded you frequently that it was important to develop your skills. When you applied for your first job, you became aware of just how important your skills were to your employer. When you started working, you probably paid very close attention to your skills. As time goes on, it will be just as important to continue to develop your skills on the job by working at them consistently, just as you did in school. By now you may have realized that learning never stops. It is a lifelong process in which new skills are identified and developed as they are needed.

As you become more familiar with your job, your efficiency in performing your duties should increase. You will most likely begin to develop new skills, too — sometimes without even being aware of it. As you know, there are skills that come more easily to some people than to others. Your employer wants you to do well. It is in the company's best interests for you to perform your job well, and it will make you feel good about yourself, too. Many companies are so concerned about improving their employees' skills, both technical and personal, that they provide on-the-job training programs for their staff.

If you are a co-op student, the company you work for is committed to helping you become the best at what you have chosen to do. If you do well, you may be offered a full-time position. The company benefits by training you in the way that will best help the firm, and the employer gets a chance to "look you over" before taking you on as a permanent, full-time employee. In any case — whether you stay on for full-time work, leave to return to school, or decide to try another position — you will have learned more about yourself and the skills you have to offer to a prospective employer.

Some companies provide financial assistance to employees so that they can take courses outside the job. This is usually done for employees who have a good record and who have been employed by the company for a prescribed length of time. The courses, which are intended to develop employees professionally or personally, are approved by the company because it feels that they will help employees improve their performance and effectiveness on the job. Whether they are college or university courses, special seminars, or on-site training sessions for certain departments, these courses are valuable to employees who wish to improve professionally and are offered at little or no cost to employees.

Some companies offer special employee assistance programs to help employees deal with personal and work-related problems that affect their physical or mental health. The programs may deal with any or all of the following issues:

- personal and emotional problems

- family relationships

- single parenting

- marital or other relationships

- stress (including job-related)

- vocational and career problems

- interpersonal relating

- financial and legal problems

- alcohol and drug abuse

These employee assistance programs usually provide voluntary, confidential counselling and referral services for employees and may also include family members. The company that provides these programs wants to make sure that the needs of its employees are met before minor problems become more serious difficulties. When employees need assistance, they are encouraged to seek help in the hope that counselling will resolve problems before they begin to affect job performance. Usually such programs are offered outside the workplace to maintain confidentiality for the employees.

Sometimes these programs are free for employees. In other cases there may be a set number of sessions offered at no cost, but if long-term or specialized assistance is necessary, employees are referred to an appropriate professional or community agency. The fees in these cases may be the responsibility of the employees or may be covered through a health-insurance plan.

Setting Goals

Whether you are at the stage of thinking about a promotion or new position or are simply concerned about doing a good job in the position you have now, it is important to identify both your strong skills and those that need to be improved. Using this information, you can develop a plan to prepare yourself for evaluation by your employer.

First you need to re-examine yourself. Take another look at yourself by referring to the "Personal Inventory" in Chapter 2. Do an updated self-inventory. Ask yourself, "What new skills have I acquired?" If you have difficulty identifying them, ask your employer or teacher to help you. Then set some goals for yourself and draw up a schedule to reach them.

To Do

1. Start by dreaming a little. Ask yourself, "Where do I want to be at the end of this year? In two years? Five years? Ten years? Twenty years?" (Later, Chapter 10 may help you re-evaluate your goals.) Write down your thoughts.

2. Next, write down what you need to do in order to be where you want to be at each time period.

3. Determine which goals are long-term and which are short-term.

4. Which goals are realistic? Which ones are unrealistic?

5. What skills do you need to develop in order to meet your goals?

6. Identify the obstacles to meeting your goals. How will you overcome them? Think about this carefully!

7. Discuss your thoughts and notes on these points with a fellow student at school and with a co-worker on the job. What new insights have you gained?

The other thing to keep in mind about setting goals is what your employer expects of you — what skills does the company expect you to have mastered, and when does it expect you to have mastered them? This is important for you to know if you are to evaluate your progress accurately and draw up a plan of action to improve your skills on the job. Once you have decided where you want to go and how to get there, don't slack off! Remember that being partway there isn't the same as being all the way there. Don't make excuses for yourself; keep going until you reach your goal, one step at a time. Stop every once in a while to evaluate your progress, and readjust your plan as needed to meet the goals you have set for yourself.

Dear Gabby:

I never thought I would be the one to write you, but I need your advice. Every year I make New Year's resolutions. All my friends ask me why I even bother, because I can never keep them. I really would like to prove to them (and to myself) that I can make some plans and stick to them. What should I do? Can you help me with my problem?

Worried in Wolfville

Dear Worried:

Think back to previous years when you made your resolutions. What kinds of resolutions did you make? Maybe they were too big to handle or not specific enough for you to really work on consistently. Did you make a plan to meet the goals you set for yourself, including how you were going to do the things you wanted to do? Did you think about how long it would take you to achieve your goals? Did you identify the obstacles that would keep you from keeping your resolutions? If so, did you plan ways to overcome the obstacles?

Perhaps your goals were too general. Sometimes we need to set very specific, small goals along the way that lead to accomplishing bigger ones later on. That way, we can see progress as we meet daily goals successfully.

Why not make only one New Year's resolution this year—to set specific, clear goals with reasonable time limits. The saying, "Success breeds success," may be true for you. As you are able to meet the simple, short-term goals, you will feel better about setting new long-term goals that will really challenge you! Go ahead and give it another try this year!

Gabby Werkes

Cases

1. Ken is always late for work. His boss has threatened to fire him if it happens again. Ken has decided always to be on time from now on.

2. Martha gained ten kilograms during the summer. She was already five kilograms overweight. She has decided to lose fifteen kilograms.

3. Jason has a habit of losing his temper at school and at work. He wants to learn to "keep his cool."

4. Wally has an essay to finish by the end of the month. He would like to finish it within a week.

5. Laura is learning to play the guitar. She wants to be ready to play in the school band by next month.

6. Jenny wants to be named "Employee of the Month" at her job. She is determined to earn this honour within three months.

7. Brett wants to buy a car in the spring. He wants to earn enough money for a down payment. He has six months to earn $4000.

To Do

For each of the above cases, decide the following:

1. Is the goal realistic?

2. Is the goal specific?

3. What are the possible obstacles to achieving the goal?

4. How could the obstacles be overcome?

Reach

5. Draw up a plan to show how the goal could be achieved, including the time needed for each of the steps in your plan.

Motivate Yourself

What makes people set goals? Why do some people set easy goals and some always set difficult ones? Why do others not seem to bother with goals at all? Where do *you* fit in?

To understand the relationship between goals and success, you need to know about motivation — that is, the need or goal that causes you to act in a certain way. Employers want their employees to be motivated toward success so that, in turn, the company will be successful. Employees want to experience success because of the self-satisfaction or other rewards they gain when their goals are achieved. The goals of new employees will likely be different from those of employees who have worked for a company for a long time. This happens because, as long-time employees reach earlier goals, they set new ones that are more challenging and rewarding.

The effort you put into achieving these goals, either personal or organizational, depends on how much they mean to you. The closer your personal goals and ideas of success are to those that your company holds, the more likely it is that you will be happy working there. A great deal of research has been done on the relationship between motivation and success, and theories have been offered to explain what success means to different people and why people behave as they do. Maslow's "Hierarchy of Needs" is one of the theories that tries to explain the needs that motivate people to achieve certain goals.

Maslow's Hierarchy of Needs

In his book *The Needs Hierarchy*, American psychologist Abraham Maslow maintained that everyone has certain needs, which Maslow arranged in a hierarchy. The basic needs were the most important ones, and Maslow arranged each level of need in order of importance. He theorized that as each level of need was met, a person would try to have the next higher level of need fulfilled. Maslow also contended that a person might move up and down the hierarchy as certain needs became dominant during that person's life.

Although he felt that his Hierarchy of Needs showed a typical pattern that operates most of the time, Maslow realized that there would be exceptions to the general tendency. For example, someone might go on a hunger strike to take a stand on a principle, thereby sacrificing a "level 1" need for a "level 5" need. To understand Maslow's theory, study the chart that follows.

Level	Need	Strength	Description of Need
1	Physiological	Strongest	These are the basic human needs to sustain life, such as food, clothing, and shelter. If these needs are not met, most of a person's time will be spent trying to meet them. A person would not be motivated by higher-level needs until these basic needs were satisfied.
2	Safety (security)	Weaker than level 1	Once the physiological needs are met, the safety needs become predominant. These needs refer to self-preservation — the need to be free from physical danger and from the fear of not having enough food and shelter for the future. When a person feels that security or safety is in danger, he or she is not concerned with the next level of needs.
3	Social (affiliation)	Weaker than level 2	Once a person's needs have been met at the first two levels, he or she will strive for meaningful relationships with others. This is the need to belong and to feel accepted by the group.
4	Esteem	Weaker than level 3	Recognition and respect from others becomes important once the lower hierarchical needs have been met. If the need for esteem is met, feelings of self-confidence, prestige, power, and control

Level	Need	Strength	Description of Need
			will result. In an effort to meet this need, a person may exhibit either positive or negative behaviour. For instance, at work an employee may behave positively by co-operating with others and earning their respect. If the employee can't satisfy the desire for attention through positive behaviour, he or she may resort to negative behaviour such as arguing with co-workers or the boss or refusing to do the work properly.
5	Self-Actualization	Weakest	Once all previous levels of needs have been satisfied, a person becomes concerned about reaching his or her potential, whatever that might be. It will, naturally, be different for each person and will depend on what is important to the individual: being a good mother, father, worker, musician, or athlete, for example.

Most people do not have to have each need completely satisfied before they feel the next level of need emerging. They may feel partially satisfied and partially unsatisfied at each level. Nevertheless, Maslow's theory can be useful in trying to predict behaviour and in understanding what motivates people.

To Do

Using Maslow's Hierarchy of Needs, determine the level of need that dominates in the following situations.

1. It is important to Trevor to be able to join the company country club.

2. Alice is a single mother and, although unhappy in her present job, won't look for another one because she has seniority and tenure where she is now.

3. Howard has just resigned from his high-paying job because of the pressure and long hours. He has taken a job that is less demanding and that will allow more time to do what he really wants, even though he will be earning 30 percent less.

4. Margaret works on an assembly line in a factory. She feels like a little cog in a very large wheel. Her work is tedious and routine, and she feels she cannot change things alone. She has decided to form a group at the factory to make management aware of the workers' sense of a lack of dignity.

5. Andre keeps pushing himself at work. He wants to "keep up with the Joneses" in his circle of friends.

6. Although Florence enjoys her job, she spends most of her spare time racing cars. She is well-known for her performance and plans eventually to enter international competitions.

Consider

Many people think that money is a great motivator. Do you agree? Why or why not? Discuss your views in class.

You Be the Judge

What do you think workers want most from their jobs?

- money
- fringe benefits
- job security
- interesting work
- promotion
- good working conditions
- feeling appreciated for the work they do

- being in control of their jobs
- an opportunity to grow

Arrange the above items in order of importance, from most important to least important. What level of need predominates in your list? Do you think managers know what employees want most? Discuss.

Dear Gabby:

My co-workers think I'm crazy. I've worked in the same department for ten years and I really like my job. My wages are okay, and I can work the hours I like, too. A new position for manager has just opened up, and everyone thinks I should apply. I really don't want the manager's job. It would mean more money and a higher position, but I'm good at what I do now and I'm not really sure that I want the extra headaches that go along with management. If I don't take it, it's not likely that I'll get another promotion. What should I do — stay happy or be harried?

Contented in Concord

Dear Contented:

If you are really happy with the way things are, don't feel that you have to fit someone else's idea of what success is. Success is attaining what you are striving for, whatever that is. It sounds like you've found it for now. If you feel differently at some time in the future, other opportunities will likely come up — if not in your present company, then outside of it. Weigh the pros and cons of the decision and then do what you believe is best for you. The path that is right for one person may not be the right path for another. It may be that you've already found yours!

Gabby Werkes

Evaluate Your Skills

Why Are Your Skills Evaluated?

The purpose of employee evaluation is to help supervisors identify the strengths and weaknesses of their employees. Assessing each worker carefully enables the supervisor to decide how best to use the skills of each person in the company

HOUSE OF MIRRORS

for the good of both the individual and the business. Often, supervisors use this information to decide who is to be promoted within the company and what positions they will be given.

Evaluation can help supervisors to know whether special training is necessary for a worker who is having trouble performing assigned tasks, or whether another job may be more suited to the worker's abilities. Proper discussion of the evaluation by the supervisor with the employees can help the employees to improve their skills and general job performance as they become more aware of their strengths and weaknesses. Proper attention to your supervisor's suggestions for improvement could result in promotion, pay raises, and better evaluations in the future.

When Will You Be Evaluated?

When you are hired, you must sometimes first complete a probationary period — a trial period to see how well you do the job. This period can be a few days or a few months in length. During this time, the employer provides you with training and makes sure that the supervisor evaluates your job skills and people skills, both of which ensure that the job is done effectively.

If you pass the probationary period successfully, you are kept on the job; if not, you are "let go." It is important to know what your employer is looking for in order to do your best in meeting the organization's objectives. If you don't do well, it is important to find out why, so that you can correct your mistakes. If you are a co-op student, it is likely that your teacher will tell you what is expected by the company before you are evaluated. Chances are that you will be more successful in meeting your employer's expectations because of the help you receive through your co-op program. You will probably adjust to the work situation more readily than those who have not had the benefit of a "coach."

After you pass the probationary period, evaluations (or performance appraisals or reviews) are conducted on a regular, ongoing basis. Some companies rate their employees once after the first three months, then at six-month intervals, and then at yearly intervals. If you are not sure when your evaluations will be done, ask, so that you can be prepared!

How Are You Evaluated?

Hardly anyone likes tests. Do you? Does it scare you when you know that you have to take a test or exam? On the job, you may be tested to measure your performance or assessed on how you perform your job on a daily basis, without taking tests.

Usually, the supervisor will check your work carefully at the beginning, correcting errors and giving suggestions to improve your work. Then after a reasonable period of time, the supervisor may arrange a time to discuss your progress, either formally or informally. The interview may be intimidating, but when you approach it positively — knowing that it is meant to provide you with constructive comments to help you do better at your job — you may actually begin to look forward to it!

During an appraisal interview, the supervisor may ask you whether you think you are progressing and ask you how you like your job. Answer this question honestly and tactfully. If you are having problems, don't be ashamed to admit it. Be specific about where you need help and perhaps even offer suggestions to your employer that would help you do your work more effectively. Be careful not to complain — keep a positive tone! If you are enjoying your job, tell your supervisor what you like most about the job. This kind of information will help your supervisor to make decisions about where and how you work best. It may determine whether you stay in the same job or are moved to another one.

Usually, when a formal performance appraisal is conducted, your supervisor will complete a form that rates your performance according to certain criteria. The information on the form will be discussed with you, and you will be asked to sign the form. Your signature does not mean that you agree with the appraisal. It simply means that you are aware of the information on the form. If you disagree with the appraisal, you may discuss your concerns during the interview or write a formal response stating your concerns, which you think should be followed up by management or the union (if one exists).

In a smaller company, the evaluation procedure may be much simpler. It may consist of a regular compliment such as "Keep up the good work!" to let you know that you are performing according to your employer's expectations.

If an evaluation form is used by your employer, before you

are evaluated you should ask to see the form. This will allow you to prepare for your evaluation because you will know the criteria being used by your supervisor. Most workers are rated on job factors such as:

- attendance

- punctuality

- ability to work with others

- quality (accuracy) of work

- quantity (amount) of work produced (production speed)

- use of time

- ability to think problems through

- initiative

- responsibility

- specific job-related skills (technical, etc.)

- willingness to follow safety rules

The supervisor may comment on each of the criteria being assessed, or simply check off a rating based on numbers or descriptors such as excellent, very good, average, fair, or below average.

If you look carefully at the above list and the following form, you will probably notice that the skills employers are concerned about are "transferable" skills, the ones that are valuable in any job. For example, the ability to work co-operatively with others is useful no matter what your job is.

Get Smart Incorporated
Employee Performance Appraisal

Employee:_____   Department:_____

Supervisor:_____   Date:_____

	Rating Scale Low High 1 | 2 | 3 | 4 | 5	Comments

1. Attendance and Punctuality
   Times Absent_____
   Times Late_____		

2. Willingness to Learn		
3. Interpersonal Skills		
4. Dependability		
5. Adaptability		
6. Job-related Technical Skills		
7. Initiative		

Short-term goals: _____

_____

_____

Long-term goals: _____

_____

_____

Supervisor's signature_____

My appraisal has been discussed with me.

Employee's signature_____

To Do

1. Look carefully at Get Smart's appraisal form. What do you think the terms mean? Are they useful criteria? Discuss your interpretation of the terms with your classmates. Do you all agree on the meaning of each of the terms?

2. Ask your supervisor for a copy of your employer's evaluation form.

   - Read it over carefully. Is it fair? Why or why not?
   - Post your evaluation form on the class bulletin board along with other evaluation forms collected by the class.
   - Discuss company evaluation forms and their fairness with the rest of the class.
   - How similar or different are the forms collected by other members of the class? Discuss the similar items on the forms. Why do various evaluation forms have some criteria in common?

3. Obtain a list of the criteria your teacher and/or supervisor will be using to evaluate your progress on the job. Compare the list(s) with the regular company evaluation form. Which things are similar? Which are different?

Reach

4. Ask your supervisor :

   - about the process of evaluation that is used at your company
   - why he or she thinks evaluation is important
   - what he or she is looking for in an employee who is
     —just starting out in a new job
     —being assessed on an ongoing basis
     —applying for promotion.

5. Discuss the results of your evaluation interview with the class. Include, as part of your discussion, your own views about employee evaluation.

6. Discuss the evaluation process used for co-op students both in school and on the job. How could it be improved? Give reasons for your statements.

7. Design an evaluation form that you would like to have used for your co-op placement. Submit it to your teacher, along with an explanation of why you included each criterion on your form.

How Do You Respond to an Evaluation?

During and after an evaluation, your response is critical. You may be used to criticism; you may even be your own best critic and put yourself down or overreact to criticism, even when it is meant to help you. But if your employer tells you that your work needs to be improved, you must remember that he or she wants you to do the best job possible. Your employer is not trying to be "mean." There is no time for pettiness in a busy employer's day. It is important for the whole company that things run smoothly, and this can be achieved when everyone works together effectively — when each person pulls his or her own weight.

How do you usually respond to criticism? Do you get angry, give up, or ignore it? Or do you try harder to do a better job the next time around? Remember that both your work and your attitude are noticed. Try to keep a positive attitude when you are corrected.

Some people have no trouble accepting criticism, but they do have a hard time accepting praise. It is just as important to be able to accept compliments about yourself or your work as it is to be able to accept criticism gracefully. When someone pays you a compliment, it is courteous and shows maturity to respond in a positive way.

To Do

How do you respond to criticism? To praise? Ask for feedback from:

- a friend
- a classmate
- your teacher
- a co-worker
- your supervisor

Self-Evaluation

Part of getting to know yourself well is the ability to see yourself in a realistic way. This means taking a long, hard, honest look at your strengths and weaknesses and trying to discover how other people see you. In evaluating yourself at work, stop from time to time to examine how you are doing. Devising a checklist or using a self-evaluation form can be a helpful way of measuring your progress. You can then compare it with the expectations of your supervisor—and determine whether you are in touch with reality!

To Do

1. Here are some sample self-evaluation questions that you could use at your job. Answering these questions honestly and finding out which areas need improvement will help you in your own growth and promotability. Try to answer them in terms of "always," "sometimes," or "never."

   Am I on time for work?
   Do I have a good reason for any absence?
   Do I dress appropriately for work?
   Do I use the telephone for business calls only?
   Am I courteous when dealing with the public?
   Am I honest about company supplies?
   Do I follow the safety rules of the workplace?
   Do I follow company rules for lunch and break times?
   Do I respect company property?

Can I keep confidences?
Do I avoid "office gossip"?
Can I be trusted?
Can I follow instructions?
Do I approach my work with enthusiasm?
Do I act on constructive criticism?
Do I use my time well?
Am I a team player?
Do I make few mistakes?
Am I complimented on my work by others?
Do I feel good about myself?
Am I willing to learn?
Do I give up easily?
Can I meet deadlines?
Am I willing to do my share of the "joe jobs"?
Am I loyal to the company?

Do this quiz from time to time to see whether you are improving in those areas that need improvement. Remember to be honest with yourself!

2. Ask your teacher, your supervisor, or a co-worker to discuss the quiz questions with you. Do they see you as you see yourself? What are your blind spots?

Reach

3. In writing, evaluate yourself on the basis of the job objectives determined for you when you started to work. Comment on your progress. Discuss how you feel about evaluating yourself.

Dear Gabby:
Today I got fired. I feel like a real failure. I'm really down in the dumps. What should I do now?

Devastated in Doomsville

Dear Devastated:

Many of us have had at least one work experience that failed. Perhaps we weren't suited to the job or were treated unfairly, or we just didn't get along with someone. You don't say what happened, but you are not the only one that has ever felt like a failure.

The reality of what has happened must be confronted in an open and honest way. Then it can be turned into a positive learning experience.

First, find someone to talk to — someone who will offer you a shoulder to cry on and who can then help you to gain a better perspective of the situation. You can't hide the bad news, and you really don't want to or need to.

Second, analyse what went wrong. If you are able to identify the problem, it may help you to make sure it doesn't happen again.

Third, start over again. A new beginning may be difficult, but it's not impossible. The only real failure occurs if you don't try again. If you want some real-life examples of how failure can be turned into triumph, read about people such as Edison, Schweitzer, and others, and companies such as 3M, which support the concept of encouragement after failure. Persistence is the key to making things work, especially after failure.

So if you're feeling discouraged, frustrated, and ineffective, just remember that all champions have been there at one time or another. You can learn from "the experts" —they are what they are because they've survived the ups and the downs along the way.

Use your personal support system and hang in there!

Gabby Werkes

Where Are You Going?

Knowing who you are and what your strengths and weaknesses are will help you to make better decisions about where you're headed, both in your personal life and in your career.

It is important to get help in assessing your abilities. You must try to determine your potential in the career you are considering, understand your limitations and how to work with them, and reflect on what you want out of life and how you intend to meet your goals.

If you are still confused about some of these things, make an appointment with a counsellor to discuss your concerns or ask questions. Get advice from experts in the field, talk to your supervisor about what he or she has learned about you during your time on the job, and take stock of yourself regularly to measure your growth.

One way to do this is to think about your work experience in depth. Make a list of all the positive things about your job. Think about why you feel that these things are positive. Then do the same with the negative aspects of your work experience. Why do you feel these things are negative? Does your list tell you anything about yourself?

Coping with changes in yourself as you mature and learn more about yourself can be both a painful process and an exciting one. How you respond to the discoveries you make about yourself is affected by your attitude toward life. It has been said that if an optimist and a pessimist were each handed half a glass of water, the optimist would describe the glass as being "half full" and the pessimist would describe it as "half empty." As you go through the stages of life and assume different social roles, you can either grow or stagnate. You can learn from your mistakes, pick yourself up, and keep going with a positive outlook, or you can throw in the towel and shuffle through life with a defeatist attitude. In the end, you yourself have a lot to do with what you get out of life.

Depending on other people or special circumstances to make you happy will lead to certain disappointment. Understanding yourself and learning how to cope with the changes that will most definitely enter your life will go a long way to ensuring a happier, healthier passage to wherever it is that you have decided to go. It is important to set goals and to know where you are headed. If you fail to do this, you won't get the sense of having "arrived." A sense of direction and a plan for getting there, combined with an adaptable outlook, are the ingredients for success.

The Changing World of Work

CHAPTER 9

The Changing World, The Changing Workplace

Your Personal Learning Objectives

After completing this chapter, you should be able to:

- Understand how *change* has been an essential part of human history.

- Understand how human progress has affected the work people do and their lifestyles.

- Identify current changes and understand how they are affecting people and the work they do.

- Predict some of the upcoming changes and developments.

- Identify the kinds of jobs that will emerge in the future.

- Identify the essential skills of the successful employee of the future.

- Describe the trends predicted for the economy and lifestyles and the resulting influences on the job market.

assembly line: a line of workers and machines along which a product is moved and assembled. Each worker or machine adds something to the product until it is completely assembled.

entrepreneur: a person who organizes, manages, and assumes the risks of a business or other financial venture.

flex hours: a system of arranging a job's timetable to suit the employee's various needs. The employee still puts in a full-time work week.

global economy: the production, purchase, and sale of goods in a world-wide market.

job sharing: a system in which one full-time job is shared by two or more employees; for example, morning hours for one employee and afternoon hours for another.

nomadic: a wandering lifestyle that involves moving from place to place in search of better hunting or grazing lands.

quality circle: a group of employees who meet regularly in order to maintain good working conditions.

Where Are We Now?

Everything is changing! By the time we learn how to use a computer program, a new, improved version becomes available. Today this is true at school as well as at the workplace. The one thing we can be very sure about in the future is that changes will continue, perhaps even more rapidly than they do today. This makes some people feel insecure, and perhaps frustrated, as they think about trying to keep up with those changes. They may complain about missing "the good old days, when..." and they tell their story and wish things would stay the same. But don't let changes make you feel uneasy.

If we look back in time, we will discover that *change* has been a constant element in history. Sometimes it is fast, sometimes slow, sometimes it is great and sometimes quite small; but change is always present.

We can trace the significant changes that took place in human development and progress over the centuries. For thousands of years, humans lived a nomadic lifestyle. Then, learning to work the land, plant crops, and raise animals allowed people to settle down in one place. Although it seems like a simple change, it took thousands of years to come about. Trade and commercial activities developed over time as a result of these settled lifestyles, but "industrial" activities were small-scale.

Then, around 1750, the Industrial Revolution drastically changed the way people lived. Factories produced more products more quickly than before. Machines and the assembly line changed the nature of human labour. More and more people were educated in schools instead of at home and on the job. Hospitals were set up to take care of the sick. People began to use the new technology to gain a better lifestyle.

Now, only two hundred years later, we are in the middle of another revolution. The "high-tech" computer age finds us replacing the factory worker with automated, computer-run assembly lines. One person using a computer today can do the work of dozens of factory workers.

Consider

1. What effect will computer technology have on the number of employees needed to do a job in the future?

2. How will work be performed in the future?

3. What kinds of jobs will be available?

4. What will employees of the future be like? What skills will they need?

Where Might You Go?

Keep the preceding questions in mind as you read the following pages. They discuss some of the changes taking place today and examine some trends for the future.

Technological Changes

Some of the most amazing and rapid technological changes have taken place in the areas of transportation and communication. Telephone communication has made remarkable strides since the telephone was invented over one hundred years ago. International long-distance calls are possible in the time it takes to dial. Teleconferencing allows groups to hold meetings over the phone, saving them travel time and expense. Computer modems make use of the telephone services to interconnect computers. Recently, the facsimile machine ("fax") has revolutionized the communication of printed materials. In seconds, a letter or a book can be transmitted thousands of kilometres.

The Jetsons, the TV cartoon "family of the future," had a marvellous telephone. They could see the person they were talking to on a monitor. When "The Jetsons" was first broadcast in the late 1960s, the possibility of having these telephones in homes seemed far away, but not anymore. They are available now at some electronics stores. But before you buy one, ask ask yourself whether you will be ready to face your caller!

Alvin Toffler, an American "futurist," writes about our changing times in his book, *The Third Wave*. He notes how fast the changes are happening. He calls the big changes we spoke of earlier "waves." The first wave, the agrarian revolution, took thousands of years. It was many thousand years again until the second wave, the Industrial Revolution, occurred. But it has taken only two hundred years for the third wave, the age of computers, to arrive.

To Do

1. What will the "fourth wave" consist of? Write a list of possible developments and discuss them in class.

2. How soon will the "fourth wave" occur?

3. If you are working, ask your employer and co-workers what trends they think will occur in their fields in the future. Share these opinions with the class.

Reach

4. If you're still curious about what Alvin Toffler has to say, go to the library and find out more about his predictions of what life will be like in the future.

5. Find out about other writers who have an interest in technology and the future. Prepare a report about these people and their ideas. Present these ideas to the class, and see what other students' reactions are to the possibility of these predictions actually coming true.

As advances in communication and transportation "shrink" our world, more people and places come within our reach. This is having a impact on the global economy, as trade and production among countries become more interdependent.

Think about the " global car" in the following illustration. It's very exciting to think of such a car being produced to include all the best components from all over the world!

Consider

1. What effect do the multiple sources of materials have on the price of the "global car"?

2. Is there a demand for such a car?

3. Based on your answers to questions 1 and 2, describe all the possible jobs involved in designing, manufacturing, and marketing this car. Describe the process as a story told by the car or by the people involved in its creation.

Reach

4. What other such "global" products might be available in the future?

Further evidence of our rapidly changing world is apparent in the language and vocabulary we use. Dictionaries are constantly making revisions by adding new words and phrases as they become used and understood by more people. Here are a few words and phrases that have been in existence for only a short time.

biogenetics   byte
electron microscope   fax
fibre optics   laser
microchip   microengineering
robotics   space station
superconductor

To Do

1. Which of the above words are familiar?

2. Find out what these words mean.

3. Make a list of five other new words you have heard of, and record their meanings.

4. Share your list with your classmates. How many of their new words are you familiar with?

5. What does the rapid development of new words and phrases mean for the worker today and in the future?

6. What would you recommend to ensure that workers are able to understand changes in their jobs?

Communicating and sharing information is and will continue to be a necessary survival skill. Rapid advances in industry have changed the world as we know it, and everyone is feeling the effects. These new developments make it faster and easier to do many things: communicate with others, produce more work in less time, and even to entertain ourselves. New technology is changing the work environment, where computers and robots are doing the jobs once done by people.

As new ideas and information develop, you may find that you need to retrain. For example, cashiers and mechanics have had to be retrained in recent years. In supermarkets, as product code scanners replaced traditional cash registers, cashiers were taught the meaning of product codes and were trained to use scanners properly. Mechanics who were licensed before electronic-control systems became common in automobiles have had to be retrained in electronics.

Consider

Talk to your employer about these things:

1. Will the future really be so different?

2. Will the jobs you are training for today exist tomorrow?

3. Will the skills you are learning today be obsolete in ten years? Why or why not?

4. Will robots and computers make workers unnecessary? Will they cause unemployment?

If you prepare for your career, you should be able to relax about your future. Certainly the new, high-technology changes will have their impact, but they will create many jobs that today do not even exist; for example, robotics repair. It is believed that most of the workforce will be working at jobs very similar to those of today, including jobs in the growing fields of health and personal services and the technical and trade areas.

No one can know for sure what jobs will exist in the year 2000, but economists are making some predictions based on statistical information. At Statistics Canada, labour-market analysts suggest that although "high tech" is getting a lot of publicity, the real employment growth will be in the service industries. Service industies are those that support the needs of people, such as transportation and communication, medical and health occupations, personal services (barbers, hairstylists, etc.), sales personnel, and the rapidly expanding food preparation, hotel, and leisure industries.

No doubt you are curious about how your job skills will fit into the future job market. How can you be trained for a future job when you are not really sure what the job will be? Your best strategy is to ensure that you get a good education now, while you are in school. Most employers look for employees who are willing and know how to learn.

As technology continues to advance, the employee who is responsible, flexible, and willing to learn and be retrained will be the most appealing to employers and the most successful.

Social Changes

Whatever type of work you do in the future, your workplace will reflect non-technological, social changes as well. They include job sharing, flexible working hours, and quality circles. These changes have benefited both companies and their employees.

Job sharing allows two or more people to share one full-time job.

Flexible working hours allow employees to adjust their start and stop times but still fulfil a full-time schedule. "Flex hours" allow employees greater flexibility in day-care arrangements, in furthering their education or training, and in commuting before or after "rush hours." At businesses where flexible working hours are possible, workers say they are happier because they feel valued by their employers. The employers are pleased because employees tend to be more productive and interested in their company.

Another improvement in the workplace is the introduction of *quality circles*. These are groups of workers who meet regularly on company time to discuss company problems. Any employee may offer suggestions or raise concerns for the quality circle to deal with. Over one hundred Canadian businesses using this system report improved production and better worker morale.

Consider

1. Why do quality circles increase the morale of employees?

2. Would you want to work in a company using this kind of system? Why or why not?

Reach

3. Many companies around the world have established other innovative programs and policies to benefit their workers. What other work-improvement programs are in operation?

Self-Employment

Being your own boss, or a "sole proprietor," is another of the developments gaining popularity. Sole proprietorships were discussed in detail in Chapter 6. Although they have some very real risks, there are also definite advantages. Over 1.5 million businesspeople in Canada are self-employed, and the number is growing annually.

- In 1975, 864 000 workers in Canada were self-employed (7 percent of the workforce).

- In 1986, 1.6 million workers in Canada were self-employed (8.3 percent of the workforce).

- In 1989, it was estimated that one in seven workers in Canada was self-employed (more than 14 percent of the workforce).

Read these charts for some other interesting statistics about self-employment.

Self-Employment: Male and Females According to Areas of Employment, 1986

Job area	% of males self-employed	% of females self-employed
1. Managerial & administration	44.5	6.9
2. Natural science / mathematical engineering	2.3	—
3. Teaching	—	2.5
4. Medicine & health	14.1	3.0
5. Artistic, literary, recreational	3.2	5.3
6. Clerical	0.5	5.1
7. Sales	16.3	19.6
8. Services	6.3	40.8
9. Farming	20.5	8.4
10. Conventional trades	22.1	0.9

Self-Employment: Age Breakdown, 1986

Ages	Percentage of population self-employed
15-34	15.6%
35-64	35.3%
65 +	49.1%

Source: Statistics Canada, 1986.

Discuss in class: What are some of the advantages and disadvantages of running your own business?

Being your own boss requires certain qualities and skills. Here are some questions you will want to answer in preparing your business proposal.

- Are you dedicated?

- Are you well-organized?

- Are you willing to work hard at something you like?

- Are you willing to take risks?

- Do you have an idea of what you will produce?

- Is there a need for your product or service?

- Where?

- Can you make a living at this?

- How will it affect your lifestyle?

- What if your business fails?

Even if you decide to "go for it," remember that local and provincial government laws and regulations will apply to your business. Investigate these laws and regulations as part of your preparation.

Financial considerations will need to be dealt with.

- Do you have start-up money?

- Are other funds available?

- Have you checked government-sponsored incentive programs to help you start up? (Funds may be available if your proposal is considered workable.)

- How will you ensure that you will make a profit?

Remember that this venture will be your means of supporting yourself and perhaps others. You will have to set up an accounting system to keep track of your income and expenses.

If, after thinking about these questions, you're still willing to go into business for yourself, think about how you will let people know what you have available for them. No matter what sort or promotion you do, your best advertising is the quality of your product or your service. And the way many people become aware of your product or service is by word of mouth, especially from satisfied customers.

Still interested? Don't let the details scare you. Your enthusiasm and hard work will pay off, as long as you are willing to make the commitment.

To Do: Try Your Wings

1. In a group of two to four of your classmates, prepare to start up your own business. Work through the above section again and answer the questions that were posed.

2. Prepare a proposal for your class as if they were considering you for a special program grant.

3. Consult a local bank manager and his or her assistant, and invite them to listen to the proposals your class feels would be "good bets." Ask them to give their opinion and to explain their reasons.

Reach

4. Invite some local entrepreneurs to sit on a panel that will evaluate your proposals and share their insights and experiences in starting a business.

Making the Workplace Workable

All these career and work developments promise some very exciting future work options and arrangements for us. But are you feeling somewhat lost in the whirlwind of it all? You are not alone! Consulting organizations have recognized that some employees want more information and guidance. They are devoting themselves to the concern for the quality of life now and in the future. They provide consultations for employees needing relief and for employers wanting to assist their employees with special programs.

The Sun Life Insurance Company became an innovator by starting the exercise break, which encouraged employees to incorporate some physical activity into their work routine. This break boosted the morale and alertness of the employees. It has expanded into various lunchtime walking and sports activities, and even into helping other companies set up their own activity programs.

Safety and comfort are also real work issues. Many companies are now considering issues such as the following: Is the physical environment a pleasant one? Is it a safe one? Are the colours of the surroundings amiable? Is the furniture comfortable? How does the lighting affect employees? Sometimes the brightness and hum of flourescent lights can cause mysterious headaches in employees, disrupting their work and lowering the morale of those working with them. These are important issues not only for the employee but also for the employer, as work efficiency improves with an improved environment.

Another problem can arise for self-employed people who work on computer terminals at home. Depression sometimes occurs when they become isolated and feel out of touch with the rest of the world. One self-employed man who lived in a high-rise condominium in Toronto reported that he hadn't been outdoors for two weeks!

Dear Gabby:
I never thought I'd be writing to a help columnist! At the age of twenty-seven I thought I had it made. I went into the accounting business for myself...one man, one computer. I decided to operate the business from my condominium and visit clients only when necessary. I had everything I needed at home. At first I thought it was terrific not having to drive into an office every day and fight traffic. I thought setting my own hours would be great; and it was, most of the time.

Recently my business has really picked up. I feel great about being able to do more than just make ends meet, but it does take up more and more of my time, so I don't get out too much. So what's my problem? I'm not sure really, except that I don't feel as happy any more about being at home all the time. I haven't spoken to anybody else about this since I feel like a spoiled kid complaining when I really have it so good. Do you have any ideas?

Lon Lee Atthome

Dear Lon Lee:
Your situation is not as rare as you think. It is not unusual for people who work at home to feel cut off from the rest of the working world (and sometimes from their friends).

You describe typical symptoms of not feeling happy, especially when you think you should. It's true that working at home can be very convenient, but what we must beware of is keeping ourselves from meeting with other people regularly. You did not say what you do for recreation. Your recent enthusiasm for your new-found business may have you neglecting that essential part of your life. As your business becomes increasingly successful, it is sure to take up more of your time.

Congratulations on your success, but perhaps it's time to share the load and hire some help. You might even feel you are ready to return to the hustle and bustle by opening a business office away from home. It could still be close by, and as the boss, you could still regulate your own hours. Have your hired help open the office early if this is necessary to your business.

You do have many options, and a good business consultant could explore others with you. But for now I think the best thing you can do is rejoin the world and have some personal contact.

Gabby Werkes

Employee unhappiness can come from many sources. Here's another letter to Dear Gabby. Have you, or has someone you know, felt this way? Compare your solution with Gabby's advice.

Dear Gabby:

I'm just starting work, and as a new graduate I'm really excited about all the opportunities coming my way. Being new, however, I get changed from area to area, and sometimes I even get loaned to other departments. I really want to do well where they send me, but so much newness really gets me feeling frazzled sometimes.

By the time I get home after a day like this (it's getting to be most days), I'm so "hyper" that I can't stop, and I feel so exhausted that all I want to do is go to sleep. This would be bearable if I could fall asleep, but for the first time in my life this is difficult. I don't know what to do! What's wrong with me?

Biz E. Jones

P.S. I really do love my job, and I don't want to change yet!

Dear Biz:

It sounds like you have some work stress to get rid of. It's natural to feel stress from the excitement of a new job and the demands we put on ourselves to do very well. The fact that you are being loaned to other areas and departments is a good indicator of your employer's confidence in your abilities, so you can ease your mind on that account.

When you enter a new area, allow yourself some time to learn the ropes, and don't be afraid to ask questions or ask for help from others. They won't think any less of you, and they may feel flattered that you are asking for their advice.

If you still feel "hyper" when you get home, try relaxing with some pleasant music, a book, or some other quiet activity to help you unwind. A warm bath has been known to work wonders before you go for that good night's sleep. Good luck and sweet dreams.

Gabby Werkes

To Do

Discuss in class what other situations can cause discontent, unhappiness, and unpleasant stress at work. Then discuss the kinds of solutions that might be possible.

All sorts of the changes we are routinely subject to can breed stress. As a member of the future workforce it will be essential to your survival and your success that you know how to deal with it. More about this in Chapter 10.

As employer and employee awareness grows about the importance of the quality of our working conditions, more businesses are adding a wide variety of employee assistance programs. Ask about the ones available at your place of work. If you don't find any, think about programs that might be useful at your workplace, and perhaps you could suggest some!

The Changing Worker

After completing this chapter, you should be able to:

● Understand the nature of change.

● Define stress and recognize the signs of stress.

● Understand how to manage stress.

● Understand predictable milestones you will face in your adult life.

● Develop a plan of action for coping with the external and internal changes that will affect you.

Key Words

milestone: originally a stone placed near a road to mark the distance to a destination; now used to mean an important event, development, or turning point.

stereotype: an oversimplified or conventional image of a certain person, group, or issue.

Change

Change scares some people. Others thrive on it and think it is very exciting. Some changes are hardly noticeable and, as a result, seem less traumatic. For example, you can't see someone age minute by minute, so you may not be aware of it. But when you see someone you haven't seen for several years, the changes are more obvious. Other changes can be catastrophic and are immediately noticeable; an earthquake can change things drastically in only minutes.

Internal changes — those changes that take place inside of us — can be either gradual or sudden, too. Some of them are desirable; others we would just as soon do without. Regardless of whether it is internal or external, the process of change is usually the same. How we deal with it will determine how we ourselves are changed by it.

To understand the nature of change, think for a moment about an ice cube. If you want to change the shape of ice from a cube to another shape, you must first melt the cube to its water state and then refreeze it in the new desired shape. It is the melt-down stage that is the most traumatic: the stage of change that requires the breakdown of the matter in order for change to occur. If you think of yourself as an ice cube going through this process, you can understand how change can make you feel uneasy. To be at this stage is to be in transition. You aren't where you were, yet you're not where you are going to be, either. You may feel very vulnerable at this point. Learning to cope with this vulnerability is a very necessary survival skill, especially in today's fast-paced society.

Stress

Have you ever felt "stressed out," burned out, uptight, excited, anxious, keyed up? Many things in life can cause you to feel stress. Not being able to cope with change effectively is one of them. It is hard to be completely free of stress. How you handle stress can mean the difference between having it work *for* you or *against* you.

Donna, for example, is a professional singer. Before a performance, she feels nervous and excited; she says that this

tension works *for* her. It gives her "an edge" that improves her concentration and vocal control. Sharma, on the other hand, feels as though she will fall apart when she has to get up in front of a crowd to give her school speech. She gets so nervous that her heart begins to pound and her palms become sweaty. She stammers and wishes she were invisible.

What is extremely stressful for one person may not be stressful for another. If you were in the same situation as Donna or Sharma, how would you react?

Stress can be caused by positive events as well as negative ones. When life changes occur, people often display signs of stress. Prolonged stress can cause a change in one's health. Here are some common ways that people feel and act when they are under stress.

aggressive
angry
antisocial
can't concentrate
can't eat
can't sleep
confused
cry
depressed
desire to escape
desire to give up
dizzy
eat too much
fearful
forgetful
general aches and pains
headaches
indecisive
irritated
jumpy
laugh uncontrollably
nervous
panicky
soreness and stiffness in muscles
tired
upset stomach

Case

David is late for work again. This time his car has run out of gas. It is pouring rain, and he has had to walk for over an hour to find a gas station. No one offered him a ride, and now he is soaked to the skin. His boss had been counting on him to arrive early to get the conference room ready for a special meeting and take some invited guests for a company tour. He is so angry that he feels like pushing his car over a cliff. He knows his boss will be upset. David feels a severe headache coming on and is feeling sick to his stomach.

Consider

1. What signs of stress is David experiencing?

2. How could the stressful situation have been avoided?

3. How should David deal with the situation now?

Stress on the job is hard to avoid, and it can get you down. If you learn how to handle it, your job will be more enjoyable and you will likely be more productive. Many people do not recognize the signs of stress and do not know how to deal effectively with stress in their lives.

Consider the following statistics, compiled by the Canadian Institute of Stress:

- Two million Canadians suffer from high blood pressure.

- Over one million Canadians regularly experience insomnia.

- Canadians have forty million prescriptions for tranquillizers filled annually.

- Premature employee death costs Canadian industry $1.9 billion a year, more than the combined 1978 profits of Canada's "top ten" companies.

- Alcoholism costs Canadian industry about $1.6 billion annually, and mental disorders cost about $1.4 billion, due to absenteeism and treatment costs.

- About 3.2 million work days and $560 million in wages and benefits are lost annually because of heart-related diseases in Canada.

- Stress and related psychosomatic problems account for as much as 80 percent of the problems treated by family doctors.

Other studies show that stress may be linked to the use of tobacco, marijuana, alcohol, and drugs.

Fact or Fiction?

Here are some statements about stress. Some are fact, others are fiction. Can you correctly identify which is which?

1. Those who feel good about themselves are not as likely to experience stress as are those who have a low self-concept.

2. These who know and accept their strengths and weaknesses are in a better position to deal with stress than those who do not.

3. Passive people, who see their fate as being determined by others, are more likely to feel stress than those who think they are in control of things.

4. Noise can be a source of stress, both physically and psychologically.

5. Pleasant surroundings can decrease stress.

6. Exercise can help to relieve stress symptoms.

7. Tension is natural.

8. Feelings of stress can be overcome by setting priorities and sticking to them.

9. Having fun relieves stress.

Answers:

1. Fact
2. Fact
3. Fact
4. Fact
5. Fact
6. Fact
7. Fact
8. Fact
9. Fact

Dear Gabby:

I am a co-op student who works as a salesperson in a busy shoe store. When I first started here, I really liked it. Now everything has changed. My boss expects me to look after the store when she goes on her breaks and lunch with the rest of the regular staff. Sometimes too many people come in at once, and I can't look after them all — I come unglued.

For instance, today a lady brought in her little brat, Tommy. He wanted cowboy boots. While I was trying to fit him, I was interrupted by another customer wanting to return a pair of shoes. When I turned my attention away, Tommy kicked me in the shins. I grabbed his foot, but he was able to kick me with the other one as he was sitting down.

Meanwhile, the lady who wanted to return the shoes that she'd worn "only once" was getting impatient waiting for me. When I finally got to her, I saw that the shoes had been worn "only once" all right — all year and never taken off! Our store policy wouldn't allow me to take them back. She yelled at me in front of a long line of customers. She said she was going to call head office and report me for being uncooperative and slow. It's so unfair! I wanted to yell right back at her and walk right out of the store.

I can't take it anymore!

Tense in Toronto

Dear Tense:

Expressing your bottled-up tension to a sympathetic ear can be incredibly helpful in relieving it. However, you will still need to reach a solution to the real problem that is causing your frustration. Take a positive attitude and go to your boss. Tell her that you want to do a good job but are unable to do so when you are left alone in the store at busy times. Ask if she can work out a more reasonable lunch and break schedule with your co-workers.

Maybe you could also suggest to your teacher that there should be a class discussion on how to deal with stressful situations. Maybe other co-op students feel the same way about things at their job, too, and need to talk about the things that bug them. Why not talk to your teacher about it?

Gabby Werkes

Identifying Stress

It is important to understand what things cause stress in your life. Once you know what they are, you can do something about them. You can try to change the situation or change yourself to make things better. Take this self-test to decide which of these things cause you to feel stress:

Myself:

- I don't like my job.

- I don't like school.

- I don't feel that I'm a good worker.

- I'd rather be doing something other than what I'm doing.

- I don't exercise much.

- I eat too much.

- I don't like the way I look.

- I don't like the way I act a lot of the time.

Foreclosure of mortgage or loan	30
New responsibility at work	29
Children leaving home	29
Trouble with in-laws	29
Great personal achievement	28
Spouse begins or stops work	26
Beginning or finishing school or college	26
Change in living conditions	25
Change in personal habits	24
Trouble with the boss	23
Change in working conditions	20
Change in residence	20
Change in school or college	20
Change in recreation	19
Change in church activities	19
Change in social activities	18
Moderate mortgage or loan	17
Change in sleeping habits	16
More or fewer family meetings	15
Change in eating habits	15
Holiday	13
Christmas	12
Minor violations of the law	11

Handling Stress

Now that you have identified some of the things that cause you to feel stress, think about how you have usually handled these feelings or situations in the past. Do you:

- worry about them?

- feel unable to do anything about them?

- get frustrated?

- get angry?

- ignore them, hoping they will go away?

- try to get even?

- take drugs or alcohol because you think it makes you feel better?

- take it out on others?

- react unpredictably?

- ask others to help?

- stay calm?

- try to think carefully about what you will do?

- try to handle things on your own?

- Other:

People handle stress differently. Some ways of handling stress are better than others. Examine the list above. Which ways work better than others? Why? Which ways don't work well? Why?

If you want to manage stress effectively, here are some ways to tackle it:

1. If you have decided that the problem is within yourself, try to change the way you look at things. Get the opinions of other people to help you see things from a different point of view. Take a positive attitude toward changing yourself. Make a list of how you would like to change and then write down ways in which you intend to meet your goals. Start with the easy changes first and work up to the ones that will take you longer to deal with. Be realistic — remember that success breeds success.

2. If you think that the source of stress is the situation, try to think of ways in which the circumstances might be changed. Make a list of things you feel can be changed, and another list of things that you believe cannot be changed. Begin to act on the things that you feel you can change. Get rid of whatever you can that is making you feel tension. If you begin to feel helpless about the things that you feel are causing pressure, talk it out with someone you feel can help to change the situation.

   For example, if you feel that too many people are assigning you tasks before you can finish previous ones, talk with your supervisor. Perhaps a different procedure could be implemented to help streamline the work, or perhaps a new structure could be set up so that you would report to fewer people. Your supervisor may have other solutions that you have not thought about, but nothing will happen until you take the first step in trying to help change things.

3.   Always take time to think things through before reacting to stress. Think about the choices you have. Approach solutions in an organized way. It may help to write things down. Often seeing things on paper gets rid of some of the panic you may be feeling. Break things down into small parts, and take one step at a time.

When you feel that you are losing control, you may experience a "block." It is hard to get started because the job seems too big; it looks overwhelming. Students sometimes feel this when beginning a special project or essay at school. Workers may experience it when approaching a seemingly impossible task. One trick in handling this type of block is to imagine that the job is done and that you are being congratulated on its success.

With a positive frame of mind, decide which things have to be done first and begin to do them. As you see things being accomplished, the feeling of stress will disappear and you will be able to finish the task more easily.

4.   Take a look at your lifestyle. Certain patterns or habits may affect your ability to handle events that are outside your control. Identify any habits you have that make you more susceptible to stress. If you regularly do some of the following things, you may be making it harder for yourself to cope:

● Do you spend a lot of time watching TV? Although this can be relaxing for some people, watching too much TV means that you may not be using your time for other outside hobbies or interests or getting the exercise that would be better for you. It may also mean that you are not doing some of the things you should be doing. Think about it for a moment — how important is TV to you? How much time do you actually spend watching TV (per day, per week)? How would you feel if you were told that you could not watch TV for the next year? If you panic at this thought, you may be spending far too much time making TV-watching a priority. Also, what you watch on TV can affect your stress level. Some people feel uncomfortable watching horror shows because of the stress they feel. A steady diet of violence can also affect your stress level.

- Do you eat the wrong foods? Foods that are high in sugar, such as candy, soft drinks, and sweet desserts, make some people nervous and jumpy. Drinks that have a high caffeine content, such as coffee, tea, and chocolate, may at first stimulate you, but they may let you down with a crash, especially if you have several cups every day. Processed foods contain chemicals that make some people tense and nervous. Alcohol can also have a negative affect in the long run if it is used to handle stress.

- Do you smoke cigarettes? People who smoke may do so because they are tense or because it has become a habit. Smoke harms the body, and the nicotine in tobacco can make a person feel even jumpier.

- Do you pay improper attention to your activities? If you stay up too late at night, you may not be getting enough sleep to let you relax after tension-filled days. Try to plan your activities so that they are well-spaced from one another, so that you don't have too many late nights in a row. Plan to set aside time for activities that you enjoy. Have fun! Keeping your life interesting and enjoyable can help you keep your mind off stressful situations.

    Getting away from routine by taking a well-de-served vacation or by having outside interests will keep you from becoming bored. On the other hand, you may be the type of person that takes too much on.

You may need to re-examine your priorities so that you do not become pressured by too many responsibilities and obligations. Be realistic. Don't expect so much of yourself.

5. If all else fails, your only solution may be to withdraw from the situation. If your boss is getting on your nerves at work and you can't cope with it, you may have to find another job. The more severe the situation, the more radical the action that may be required. This may take real effort, but it may be necessary.

Cases

Read the following cases. After giving careful thought to each one, do the following:

1. Discuss them with a classmate or a co-worker.

2. Evaluate what could be done to change the situation.

3. Explain how the people mentioned in the cases could change themselves or their outlook to ease their stress.

1. Dan works in a busy woodworking shop. He often feels pressured with his work because he has trouble meeting the deadlines that his boss sets. He wishes that his boss wouldn't promise customers that the work will be done "right away." Dan sometimes wonders whether he is just too slow to handle the work. What would you do if you were Dan?

2. Francine is always being criticized by her boss for not doing her job right. He accuses her of making mistakes and of not being enthusiastic about her job. Francine feels that she does a good job, but often her boss loses papers, messes up the office files, and makes promises to clients that he has no intention of keeping. Francine used to like her job, but she is tired of making excuses for her boss when he misses meetings that he hasn't told her about and of taking the blame when things go wrong. What would you do if you were Francine?

3. Logan is very hurt and angry. He has just overheard two of his co-workers discussing the new position opening up. They are talking about how Logan doesn't have a chance for the job because he has far less education than those he works with. They have worked for the company for only a year and Logan has trained them for their jobs. He is worried that he will not be considered for the position because of his low level of education, yet feels that he should get it because he has far more knowledge and experience than his co-workers do. What would you do if you were Logan?

4. Identify a stressful job situation of your own. If you are not working, identify a stressful situation in your personal life. Describe the situation. How will you handle it?

Dear Gabby:
My friends all say that I am crazy because I like to do a job well. When I am at work I enjoy the feeling I get when I meet tight deadlines and produce good work. I feel pride in my accomplishments and, when the situation demands it, will work until midnight with others in my office to get the job done right. I know that my boss appreciates my efforts, but my friends say that I'd better stop pushing myself so hard or I'll burn out. What do you think?

I. Tryhard

Dear Tryhard:
It seems that you are handling pressure on the job well. Stress can lead to burnout when a person feels overworked and yet feels that he or she contributes less and less. Morale is usually low, and the person may experience insomnia, irritation, fatigue, and other symptoms. Yet many people feel that pressure is a healthy form of stress because they do their best work when the stakes are high and their efforts are appreciated.

Stress is not necessarily negative. Without positive stress, many people would not attempt to reach their full potential.

Personal Change

Milestones

One of the most important results of change is that it changes
us. It is hard to imagine what we will be like in five years, ten
years, or twenty years. Some of us have a hard time predicting
what we will be like in just a year's time!

Fortunately the stages of development are generally predictable. When we become adults, we don't stop growing,
changing, and maturing. There are milestones that we can all
expect to reach. Knowing what these milestones are will help
us to make wise choices for our future. This section deals with
the following issues:

- Understanding the milestones you will face.

- Becoming aware of how external changes may affect you.

- Models to follow for making good decisions.

Have you ever heard of the "seven-year itch"? This usually refers to an inner restlessness that precedes change. Most people experience periods of reflection when they reach a milestone such as the death of a loved one, a promotion at work, illness, a love affair, or another event that has a sudden impact on their lives.

According to scientific studies the adult milestones, although they are generally predictable, are not reached by everyone at the same age. Rather, some people experience them before or after others, depending on their particular stage of development. How you handle yourself at each stage is determined by:

- your attitude toward the change (your readiness for change: whether or not you feel you need a change)

- your feelings about yourself (self-esteem, security)

- your relationships with other people (attitudes of and pressures from parents, friends, co-workers, teachers, and others)

- your age (how much time you think you have left to do the things you would like to do).

If you face each milestone knowing that it will bring growth, it will be easier to face those times of transition. Only you can take responsibility for and control of your life. Every choice you make as you face the difficult decisions at each milestone will shape your life. Does this sound "heavy"? It is, but remember that the decisions you make can be changed, even though there will be consequences to deal with — you do not have to be locked into one particular lifestyle forever!

No one can read your future, but Dr. Miriam Stoppard, in her book *Everywoman's Lifeguide*, has summarized the milestones you should be aware of, each one with its own lifestyle crises.

Your Twenties

- You choose a pattern for living, either one with strong commitments to what is expected of you by family, peers, or society, or one that is temporary and easily changed (you avoid strong commitments).

- You feel that the decisions you make are permanent.

- You plan ways to meet future goals and objectives, professionally and personally.

- You are more stable than you were during your adolescent years.

- You have a desire to form a permanent, intimate relationship with another person.

Your Thirties

- You re-examine the choices you made in your twenties.

- You feel that new choices have to be made and prior commitments altered or adjusted.

- You have a desire to develop a personal life with more social involvement and a sense of contributing.

- You become aware of aging and of having reached the half-way stage in your life.

- You review your life: its past choices, present situation, future options.

- You want change, which brings with it internal pressure: a choice must be made to make the change or to do nothing. This can be a turbulent time in which radical decisions are either made or deferred until later.

Your Forties

- If a desire for change has not occurred in your thirties, it may occur in your forties.

- The decisions you deferred in your thirties will resurface in your forties. If you put them aside again, feelings of resignation and stagnation may develop. Your frustration may build, and a crisis may hit hard in your fifties. If you act upon your desire for change, renewal may occur. If you make choices and adjustments and sort out your lifestyle, a feeling of contentment and self-confidence results.

- Your changes demand readjustment: your children may be leaving home, your career may become less satisfying. You make decisions that will bring about a new sense of purpose in your life.

- You establish new priorities.

- Your relationships with others change: you let your children go their own way and place more emphasis on your friendships.

Your Fifties

- Physical changes occur: your senses and mental capacities may deteriorate.

- The demands of your aging parents may be difficult to meet.

- You realize that your life may soon end.

- You re-examine your priorities in your social life, work life, and personal life. Retirement looms, along with new worries about its effect on your lifestyle. You become more reflective about life in general.

- Your pace slows down.

- Your outlook becomes more philosophical toward the end of your fifties; you become more accepting of your and others' abilities and limitations. You mellow!

Your Sixties

- Your position at work is fairly secure because of your experience and the competence you have acquired.

- The nature and scope of your activities may be curtailed by a decline in your physical or mental capabilities or by psychological factors.

- You have a tendency to let go: you hand over your responsibilities in social and professional areas to others, reduce your workload, move to a different place that requires less care, change your lifestyle for more leisure time and adjusted living costs.

- You have a greater desire to become involved in social organizations.

- Retirement: a possible change in your standard of living, use of time, professional contacts, friendships, and other radical changes.

Your Seventies and Beyond

- Your health becomes very important to you.

- You become more introspective as you think about your past life.

- You tend to cling to old friends and family and must cope with the death of friends.

- You concentrate on remaining independent, capable, and mentally alert.

- You adjust to a slower pace of life.

Coping with Change: A Plan of Action

If looking over the milestones in life has depressed you, remember that preparation makes all the difference in moving from one stage to another and that the milestones can be approached with a positive attitude. When faced with difficult decisions in your life, it helps to have an objective view of the situation and a model for dealing with change in an organized manner.

A Decision-Making Model

For any problem that you have to solve, try using these steps to help you reach a decision.

1. Study the situation (or case) carefully.

2. Identify the main problem and write it down.

3. List all the issues related to the problem.

4. Write down all possible solutions (your choices). (Don't forget "do nothing" — it, too, is an alternative.)

5. State the consequences (good and bad) of each choice.

6. Choose the best (the most realistic) alternative.

7. Write out a plan for implementing your chosen alternative. (Do this in a step-by-step format and include a timetable showing when you must complete each part of the plan.)

8. Decide how you will evaluate whether or not your plan is successful. (How will you find out whether it has worked? Who will you ask? How will you get feedback? What will you do with the feedback you receive? Will any change be required?)

Cases

For each of the following cases, use the model described above to arrive at a solution. Refer to the "Milestones" section of this chapter for additional considerations when analysing each case. Write down a solution for each case and discuss it in class, in small groups.

1. Byron is a trained heavy-equipment operator. He has always enjoyed a good income and steady work in his community. He is good at his job and has always been in demand. Now things have begun to change. Construction in his community has come to a standstill. Byron has been out of work for five months now, and he is getting worried. In order to make enough money to support his family, Byron will have to move closer to a large city three hundred kilometres away, where there is more work for him. He is forty-four years old, his wife is thirty-nine, and they have three school-age children. None of them likes the idea of moving away from home.

2. Nancy is the lead guitarist in a country music band and is on the road for months at a time. She and her husband have two young children. One day when Nancy returns home, she finds a note on the table from her husband. He has run away with her best friend and never wants to see her again. He has taken the children with him. Nancy is twenty-nine years old. She doesn't know what to do.

3. Terry is a mechanic. He works all day for a garage fifty kilometres from his home. He doesn't like it there. In the evenings and on weekends, he works on cars in his own garage at home, mostly as a favour to his friends. It gives him a bit of extra pocket money, but it's not enough to live on. He has five children, ranging in age from four to eighteen. Terry is thirty-eight years old and in his second marriage. His wife is unhappy.

4. Ned is a jeweller. He owns his own store. Business is not very good, even though Ned works long hours. He is satisfied to earn just enough to get by. His wife has a good job and brings in a good income. They like to go on holidays frequently. They have no children. Ned is in his late forties and is content. Recently, Ned's wife, in her late thirties, has decided she wants to have a family. They cannot agree.

5. Ron works in a factory. He spends a lot of his spare time singing; in fact, he has decided to cut his first album. He has three children, his wife works, and money is tight. It is a financial sacrifice for him to cut the record, but it has always been one of his dreams. His wife is supportive. Ron is thinking about quitting his job and going into music full-time.

6. Bob is in his early sixties. He worked for many years as an electrical engineer with a large company and travelled all over the world on large projects. When the company he worked for was bought out by a large conglomerate, Bob's employment was terminated. For the last ten years, Bob has worked on odd jobs out of his home. He is now having health problems and has lost the use of his right hand. His wife does not work outside of the home. They have five grown children who are living on their own and another child who is institutionalized.

7. Miriam and John met at an international convention some time ago. During the time they worked together on joint projects, they fell deeply in love with one another. They are both well educated, have good jobs, and are in line for promotion in their careers. They are both in their forties. Each is unhappily married to someone else, and each has a teenage child. Miriam and John live in different countries. They have both done a lot of soul-searching and, realizing that life is short, are considering spending the rest of their lives together.

8. Elsie is sixteen and is thinking about becoming a lawyer. She loves to read and, ever since she was eleven, has watched as many police and law TV programs as she can. Law school will be expensive, but her marks are good and her parents have always encouraged her to be whatever she wants to be when she leaves school. What Elsie doesn't know is that her father has been diagnosed as terminally ill and has only a year to live. Her parents are in a dilemma: because of the medical bills, they may not be able to pay for Elsie's further education.

9. Francesca is twenty-three and has been working for a year. She has been engaged to be married for two years. She wants to get married right away, but her parents are against it. Her fiancé still has a year left in university. This means that she will have to support him and carry the full financial load herself. Although she and her fiancé see no problem with this arrangement, they want to make the right decision.

10. Eliza has been at home raising her family for nineteen years and wants to take a job that will start in six months. The job has been offered to her by a friend, who has asked Eliza to fill in for her while she is on maternity leave. There may be a chance for the job to be extended afterwards for Eliza, if she wants to stay on. She is excited about this new opportunity, but before she can take the job she has to go back to school to update her skills. She suddenly feels terrified at the prospect of being with young people in class and wonders if she will be able to handle it. She has no self-confidence and wonders whether she can really do the job after all. She doesn't know what to tell her friend.

11. Greer has just finished her co-op placement and has changed her mind about her career. She wants to do something completely different from what she thought she wanted before her co-op program, but she's not sure what it is.

12. Margaret is eighteen and was planning to attend college in the fall. She has just found out she is pregnant. She does not want to get married, and her boyfriend has said he will not support the child. Margaret doesn't know what to do. Suddenly her whole life has changed.

To Do

1. Think seriously about how you would complete each of the following statements, write down your thoughts, and then discuss them with someone in class that you don't know very well.

   - Next year, I'll . . .
   - In five years, I'll . . .
   - In ten years, I'll . . .
   - In twenty years, I'll . . .
   - In thirty years, I'll . . .
   - In forty years, I'll . . .
   - In fifty years, I'll . . .

   Reach

2. When you die, how would you like to be remembered? Write your own epitaph.

3. Analyse your responses to the above statements. What things seem to be important to you? List your goals in life. Draw up a long-term plan for accomplishing them.

Changing Lifestyles and Workstyles

As well as considering internal personal change, you must think about external changes when trying to plan for your future. Again, there is no crystal ball to help you, but you can be certain of some trends that will affect your life.

It used to be (not so long ago!) that lifestyle choices seemed pretty limited. In fact, girls were once asked, "What do you want to be: a nurse or a teacher? Or are you going to stay home and have children?" Nowadays, the choices are much wider, and efforts are being made to get rid of the sexist stereotypes that females have traditionally been faced with. Women are able to take jobs in many areas that were usually held by men. They are being encouraged to select subjects at school that will prepare them to be capable professionals and tradespeople in whatever areas interest them.

Never before have we had so much choice in the kind of work we want to do. We can think not only about how our abilities would fit in with the demands of a particular job, but also about when we would like to work, at what, and where. Flexibility and personal choice are important considerations for more and more people as they prepare themselves for the workplace of today and tomorrow.

In the past, people thought that their lives would progress in a straight, linear way:

Stage	Pre-school	School	Work	Retirement
Age	0–5 years	5–19 years	19–65 years	65+ years

Recently there has been a change in this pattern. It affects the way in which people prepare for the future, both in their personal lifestyle choices and in work preparation.

Stage	Pre-school	School	Work & School	Work/School/Work/School/Work	Retirement/School/Work
Age	0–2 years	2–16 years	16–21 years	21–70 years	70+ years

Not only are people today in school longer and working longer, but they will go back and forth, between school and work, several times in their lives for retraining and upgrading. This new trend is called lifelong learning. More and more adults are going back to school, and more and more companies are offering on-the-job training as today's working world demands greater and more specialized knowledge.

Those who study these trends estimate that people will also change their careers (not just jobs) up to six times during their working lives. This means that the skills they learn in one job should be transferable to the next one — the generic skills will become most important. In addition to learning the three R's (Reading, wRiting, and aRithmetic), successful job candidates will need the four C's: Communication skills, Computational skills, Critical thinking skills, and Coping Skills. So, if you can hardly wait to leave school for the last time and think that you'll never go back, think again! Chances are that you are just beginning your formal education now and that it will continue all of your life! "Horrors!" you say? Think about the positive aspects of the situation: as you continue your learning and keep up to date on new equipment and methods, you open up your chances for more challenging career opportunities, keep your mind active, and make new friends along the way!

There will be new opportunities for increased pleasure as more leisure time becomes available through job-sharing programs. Jobs can be shared in a variety of ways, using flexible arrangements, in which one person covers for another in emergencies or on an on-call basis; one person works mornings, another afternoons; workers alternate days; or employees work "blocks" of time. All these choices allow workers more freedom to choose when and for how long they want to work. Some employers have leave-of-absence programs in which employees can work for a certain length of time, take time off without losing their jobs or job benefits, and then return to the same job.

Other employers allow exchanges or encourage transfers of personnel to enrich their staff and increase their staff's experience. Teachers, for example, are able to work in various countries throughout the world because some boards of education sponsor these kinds of programs.

If working around the world appeals to you, then you may choose to enrol in a course that will prepare you to work for a company in another country. Perhaps you will choose to work for a company that has branch offices in various locations and that will allow you to transfer as you follow your career path within the company. The global economy is making new opportunities available for skilled people to work in a variety of locations, learn about other cultures, and enrich their lifestyles. Working in the foreign service provides these types of opportunities; or perhaps you will be an entrepreneur who will make your own way in the working world, doing the things that you most want to do, the way you want to do them.

Whatever you choose to do, remember that you hold the keys to your future now. It is an exciting time in which to live. There are opportunities for full and enriching experiences for those who have the courage and determination to plan and work for a meaningful life.

Your work will be a large part of your life. As you go through your life and work experiences and come to terms with reality, you will have your share of rewarding and exciting encounters at each milestone. Make sure you are well prepared, and you will be ready to meet the next challenge with self-confidence and enthusiasm!

Index

industry standards for, 141
injuries, preventing, 138
refusal to work, 140-41
rules and precautions, 136-38
Self-employment, 231-34, 235
Self-image, 44
Signature, importance of, 180-81
Skills, 25, 33
    developing, 198-200
    speaking, 108-112, 116
    telephone, 114-20
    transferable, 25, 214
Skills evaluation, 209-18
    appraisal interview, 211-12
    form, 212-14
    methods of, 211-14
    reasons for, 209-210
    responding to, 215-16
    self-evaluation, 216-17
    times for, 210-11
Social Insurance Number (SIN), 92
Sole proprietorship, 156-58
Speaking skills, 108-112, 114
Stereotype, 20, 239
    defined, 4
Stress, 241-55
    blocks, 251
    handling, 249-53
    identifying, 246-48
    scale, 248-49
    statistics, 243-44
    symptoms of, 242
Structure, 152

T

Team member, becoming, 93-94
Telephone skills, 114-20
Temperament, 25, 35
Terminology, 91
Toffler, Alvin, 226
Trade Union Act of Canada, 166
Transferable skills, 25
Transition, 4, 5-6, 241

U

Unemployment Insurance Commission, 189-90
Unions, 166-77
    affiliates, 174

collective agreements, 168-71
forming, 167
local, 174-75
membership in, 167-68
national/international, 174
reasons for, 166

V

Vacancies, *see* Job vacancies
Values, 15-16
Volunteer, 4
Volunteer work, 13-15

W

Work
    ancient Greek attitude to, 7
    defined, 4, 6
    economic reasons for doing, 8-9
    full-time vs. part-time, 51-52
    during Industrial Revolution, 7
    myths about, 19-22
    as part of team, 10-11
    satisfaction with, 10
    and self-respect, 10
    as social interaction, 9
    as useful activity, 11
    volunteer, 13-15
    what it's like, 48-51
Worker's Compensation Board (WCB), 147-48
Working conditions, 155
Workplace
    ethics in, 191-92
    formal/informal rules of, 154
    quality of life, 234-38
    security in, 180-83

Y

"You" collage, 30-31